Our beautiful,
blessed family

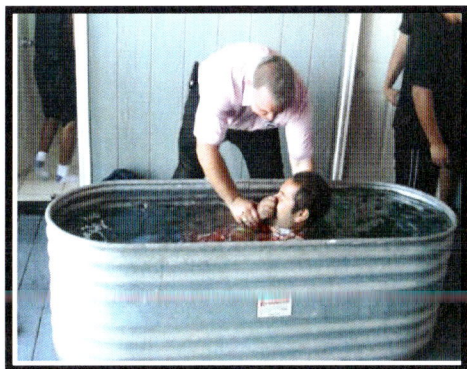

A wonderful
Baptism

What's The Bible Got To Do With It?

FORWARD

"What's The Bible Got To Do With It?" is a great question. The Bible has been given lip service as a "good book" but not "The Book" for life. When I was challenged by a question, "Are you saved?" I responded, "Uh, well, what is that?" This person answered by showing me the Biblical meaning. This truth provoked me to accept the only Saviour JESUS CHRIST. I proceeded to read and study the Bible. I was challenged to find out what the Bible says for my life. In the beginning, I began to establish a basis or foundation for my beliefs. I always wondered what the Bible said about certain questions and issues. While studying, I found out that most of "my beliefs" were not based on the Bible but upon man. With this biblical perspective, the basis for this book is who I have become for decisions in life! By the way, the person that asked me about being saved is the same person that I married. Thank you Tammy for being my precious wife and being my ears, eyes, grammar, patience, etc. throughout the hours of writing! Also, thank you to our children Kelle Jr., Kalen, Kyla, Kiery, and Kesha for letting me share my thoughts and ideas contained in this book. I love you!

What's The Bible Got To Do With It?

What's The Bible Got To Do With It?

Kelle Hein

What's The Bible Got To Do With It?

This is a thesis work by the author for partial fulfillment of the requirements for the degree, Doctor of Ministry.

All Bible references are from the King James Bible.

Shari Parker Publishing and Printing
2785 CR 3103
New Boston, Texas 75570
903-933-6273
sharipar@yahoo.com
www.shariparkerpublishingandpriting.com

ISBN 978-0-9898987-2-0

10 9 8 7 6 5 4 3 2 1

Printed in the United States of America

TABLE OF CONTENTS

What's The Bible Got To Do With It?

FACTS

Multitudes of books have been written about various topics. Basically, pick a problem and a book is probably available. Ask somebody a question and they will have an opinion, but sometimes it is the not so obvious question that needs an answer. The Bible is the premier authority and it will always be insightful for subject matter. When you have a question about a pertinent, relevant or unpopular question, where do you go? Enclosed in the Bible are some principle explanations about some miscellaneous questions in life.

> *"Let your speech be always with grace, seasoned with salt, that ye may know how ye ought to answer every man." Colossians 4:6; "But sanctify the LORD GOD in your hearts: and be ready always to give an answer to every man that asketh you a reason of the hope that is in you with meekness and fear" I Peter 3:15*

For common answers to some uncommon questions, the Bible is your reference!

AGE OF ACCOUNTABILITY- Biblical accountability is when you can give an account for understanding the consequences of sin. That age is not written in stone, however; the time will arrive when each person knows the difference. Until that age comes, babies and mentally challenged people are safe in the LORD. King David proves this truth concerning his son and the promise that he would one day see him again. The child had not yet reached the "age of accountability".

"Therefore to him that knoweth to do good, and doeth it not, to him it is sin." James 4:17;
"And he said, While the child was yet alive, I fasted and wept: for I said, Who can tell whether GOD will be gracious to me, that the child may live? But now he is dead, wherefore should I fast? Can I bring him back again? I shall go to him, but he shall not return to me." II Samuel 12:22, 23

AMBIDEXTROUS- Warriors who are efficient with both the right hand and the left hand; what a blessing!

"They were armed with bows, and could use both the right hand and the left in hurling stones and shooting arrows out of a bow, even of Saul's brethren of Benjamin." I Chronicles 12:2

ANIMAL RIGHTS- GOD said that man will dominate over animals, not vice versa.

"And God said, Let us make man in our image, after our likeness: and let them have dominion over the fish of the sea, and over the

fowl of the air, and over the cattle, and over all the earth, and over every creeping thing that creepeth upon the earth." Genesis 1:26

ARK of TESTIMONY/TESTAMENT (COVENANT, GOD)- There is an age old question about the Ark of God; its existence and whereabouts still remain unanswered or does it?

"And when Moses was gone into the tabernacle of the congregation to speak with him, then he heard the voice of one speaking unto him from off the mercy seat that was upon the ark of testimony, from between the two cherubims: and he spake unto him." Numbers 7:89; "And the temple of God was opened in heaven, and there was seen in his temple the ark of his testament: and there were lightnings, and voices, and thunderings, and an earthquake, and great hail." Revelation 11:19

ASTROLOGY-

"Which maketh Arcturus, Orion, and Pleiades, and the chambers of the south."; "Canst thou bind the sweet influences of Pleiades, or loose the bands of Orion?" Job 9:9; 38:31; "Seek him that maketh the seven stars and Orion ." Amos 5:8

SOLAR ECLIPSE- The LORD caused a total black out that could be felt. Only where the Israelites dwelt was there light!

"And the LORD said unto Moses, Stretch out thine hand toward heaven, that there may be darkness over the land of Egypt, even darkness which may be felt. And Moses stretched forth his hand toward heaven; and there was thick darkness in all the land of Egypt three days: They saw not one another, neither rose any from his place for three days: but all the children of Israel had light in their dwellings." Exodus 10:21-23

BABIES

MIDWIVES- An Egyptian position for delivering babies was blessed by GOD for saving the Hebrew male children.

"And the king of Egypt spake to the Hebrew midwives, of which the name of the one was Shiphrah, and the name of the other Puah: And he said, When ye do the office of a midwife to the Hebrew women, and see them upon the stools: if it be a son, then ye shall kill him: but if it be a daughter, then she shall live. But the midwives feared God, and did not as the king of Egypt commanded them, but saved the men children alive. And the king of Egypt called for the midwives, and said unto

them, Why have ye done this thing, and have saved the men children alive? And the midwives said unto Pharaoh, Because the Hebrew women are not as the Egyptian women: for they are lively, and are delivered ere the midwives come in unto them. Therefore GOD dealt well with the midwives: and the people multiplied, and waxed very mighty." Exodus 1:15-20

MISCARRIAGE- This is very hard to understand, but it is not foreign to the Bible.
"Or as an hidden untimely birth, I had not been: as infants which never saw light." Job 3:16

TWINS- The LORD substantiates two specific nations from two specific persons. This is very interesting for those who do not believe in life at conception!
"And the LORD said unto her, Two nations are in thy womb, and two manner of people shall be separated from thy bowels: and the one people shall be stronger than the other people: and the elder shall serve the younger. And when her days to be delivered were fulfilled, behold, there were twins in her womb." Genesis 25:23, 24

WEANING- When is the right age to wean a child? We are told in I Samuel that Hannah did not go to the yearly sacrifice until after Samuel was weaned. The scripture tells us that Hannah went to the sacrifice with her young (infancy to adolescence) child. In our day, customarily, physical and social concerns define the time, however; the LORD will establish His word for the definitive age.

"But Hannah went not up; for she said unto her husband, I will not go up until the child be weaned, and then I will bring him, that he may appear before the LORD, and there abide for ever. And Elkanah her husband said unto her, Do what seemeth thee good; tarry until thou have weaned him; only the LORD establish his word. So the woman abode, and gave her son suck until she weaned him. And when she had weaned him, she took him up with her, with three bullocks, and one ephah of flour, and a bottle of wine, and brought him unto the house of the LORD in Shiloh: and the child was young."
I Samuel 1:22-24

BASTARD- Unfortunately, humanity has denigrated a biblical word into a "swear word". The Scriptures speak about legitimate and illegitimate children. The LORD's legitimate children partake and endure chastisement; if not, they are illegitimate (bastard).

"And ye have forgotten his exhortation which speaketh unto you as unto children, My son, despise not thou the chastening of the LORD, nor faint when thou art rebuked of him: For whom the LORD loveth he chasteneth, and scourgeth every son whom he receiveth. If ye endure chastening, GOD dealeth with you as with sons; for what son is he whom the father chasteneth not? But if ye be without chastisement, whereof all are partakers, then are ye bastards, and not sons. Furthermore we have had fathers of our flesh which corrected us, and we gave them reverence: shall we not much rather be in subjection unto the Father of spirits, and live?" Hebrews 12:5-9

BLOOD- Because we are all of the same blood, racism is a foolish belief.

"And hath made of one blood all nations of men for to dwell on all the face of the earth, and hath determined the times before appointed and the bounds of their habitation:" Acts 17:26

If the scripture had been applied, blood letting would not have existed!

"For the life of the flesh is in the blood; and I have given it to you upon the altar to make an

atonement for your souls: for it is the blood that maketh an atonement for the soul." Leviticus 17:11

We are saved by the LORD's shed blood!

"And almost all things are by the law purged with blood: and without shedding of blood is no remission." Hebrews 9:22; "..Unto him that loved us, and washed us from our sins in his own blood." Revelation 1:5

"Take heed therefore unto yourselves, and to all the flock, over the which the Holy Ghost hath made you overseers, to feed the church of God, which he hath purchased with his own blood." Acts 20:28

BODY MARKINGS-

EARRINGS- They can be used as a form of idolatry for who you are or to what you can become.

"And they gave unto Jacob all the strange gods which were in their hand, and all their earrings which were in their ears: and Jacob hid them under the oak which was by Shechem." Genesis 35:4; "And Gideon said unto them, I would desire a request of you, that ye would give me every man the earrings of his prey. (For they had golden earrings, because they were Ishmaelites.)" Judges 8:24; "And I put a jewel on thy forehead, and

earrings in thine ears, and a beautiful crown upon thine head." Ezekiel 16:12

PIERCINGS-This was a way to prove servitude. If a freed slave wanted to remain under the master, a hole was bore in the ear of the slave.
"Then his master shall bring him unto the judges; he shall also bring him to the door, or unto the door post; and his master shall bore his ear through with an aul; and he shall serve him for ever." Exodus 21:6

TATTOOS- A GOD given body should be left well enough alone.
"Ye shall not make any cuttings in your flesh for the dead, nor print any marks upon you: I am the LORD." Leviticus 19:28

CANNIBALISM-
"And the king said unto her, What aileth thee? And she answered, This woman said unto me, Give thy son, that we may eat him today, and we will eat my son tomorrow. So we boiled my son, and did eat him: and I said unto her on the next day, Give thy son, that we may eat him: and she hath hid her son." II Kings 6:28, 29

CAPITAL PUNISHMENT-

> *"Whoso sheddeth man's blood, by man shall his blood be shed: for in the image of God made he man." Genesis 9:6; "He that smiteth a man, so that he die, shall be surely put to death." Exodus 21:12; "...Deliver him that smote his brother, that we may kill him, for the life of his brother whom he slew..." II Samuel 14:7*

CARDIO PULMONARY RESUSCITATION (CPR)-

> *"And he went up, and lay upon the child, and put his mouth upon his mouth, and his eyes upon his eyes, and his hands upon his hands: and he stretched himself upon the child: and the flesh of the child waxed warm." II Kings 4:34*

CREMATION-

> *"All the valiant men arose, and went all night, and took the body of Saul and the bodies of his sons from the wall of Beth-shan, and came to Jabesh, and burnt them there. And they took their bones, and buried them under a tree at Jabesh, and fasted seven days." I Samuel 31:12, 13; "And they buried him in his own sepulchers, which he had made for himself in the city of David, and laid him in the bed which was filled with sweet*

odours and divers kinds of spices prepared by the apothecaries art: and they made a very great burning for him." II Chronicles 16:14

DEATH

APPOINTED TIME- Physical life was never created for eternity. May we all understand that life is precious and short. Utilize your time wisely!

"And as it is appointed unto men once to die, but after this the judgment:" Hebrews 9:27; "Man that is born of a woman is of few days, and full of trouble. Seeing his days are determined, the numbers of his months are with thee, thou hast appointed his bounds that he cannot pass:" Job 14:1, 5; "LORD, make me to know mine end, and the measure of my days, what it is; that I may know how frail I am." "So teach us to number our days, that we may apply our hearts unto wisdom." Psalms 39:4; 91:12

ABORTION- This is still pro-death no matter how you say it or slice it!

"Thou shalt not kill" Exodus 20:13; "If men strive, and hurt a woman with child, so that her fruit depart from her, and yet no mischief follow; he shall be surely punished, according as the woman's husband will lay upon him; and he shall pay as the judges determine.

And if any mischief follow, then thou shalt give life for life." Exodus 21:22, 23;

POST BIRTH ABORTION- Selective or not, it is still murder!

"And the king of Egypt spake to the Hebrew midwives, of which the name of the one was Shiphrah, and name of the other Puah: And he said, When ye do the office of a midwife to the Hebrew women, and see them upon the stools: if it be a son, then ye shall kill him: but if it be a daughter, then she shall live." Exodus 1:15, 16

HANGING-

"But he hanged the chief baker: as Joseph had interpreted to them." Genesis 40:22; "And harbonah, one of the chamberlains, said before the king, Behold also, the gallows fifty cubits high, which Haman had made for Mordecai, who had spoken good for the king, standeth in the house of Haman. Then the king said, hang him thereon. So they hanged Haman on the gallows that he had prepared for Mordecai. Then was the king's wrath pacified." Esther 7:8, 9

MURDER- Because of pride and jealousy, one brother killed another.

"And Cain talked with Abel his brother: and it came to pass, when they were in the field, that Cain rose up against Abel his brother, and slew him." Genesis 4:8

PREMEDITATED MURDER-
"And it came to pass in the morning, that David wrote a letter to Joab, and sent it by the hand of Uriah. And he wrote in the letter saying, Set ye Uriah in the fore-front of the hottest battle, and retire ye from him, that he may be smitten, and die." II Samuel 11:14, 15

SUICIDE- This choice of death is sin! The results of guilt or remorse can drive a person to attempt or commit suicide. One's death does not determine final destiny. The body is dead but the soul lives. Being saved or lost verifies eternity!

"And at midnight Paul and Silas prayed, and sang praises unto God: and the prisoners heard them. And suddenly there was a great earthquake, so that the foundations of the prison were shaken: and immediately all the doors were opened, and every one's bands were loosed. And the keeper of the prison awaking out of his sleep, and seeing the prison doors open, he drew out his sword, and would have killed himself, supposing that the prisoners had been fled. But Paul cried

with a loud voice, saying, Do thyself no harm: for we are all here. Then he called for a light, and sprang in, and came trembling, and fell down before Paul and Silas, And brought them out, and said, Sirs, what must I do to be saved? And they said, Believe on the LORD JESUS CHRIST, and thou shalt be saved, and thy house." Acts 16:25-31

"Then said Saul unto his armourbearer, Draw thy sword, and thrust me through therewith; lest these uncircumcised come and thrust me through, and abuse me, But his armourbearer would not; for he was sore afraid. Therefore Saul took a sword, and fell upon it." I Samuel 31:4; "And the king said unto her, Be not afraid: for what sawest thou? And the woman said unto Saul, I saw gods ascending out of the earth. And he said unto her, What form is he of? And she said, An old man cometh up; and he is covered with a mantle. And Saul perceived that it was Samuel, and he stooped with his face to the ground, and bowed himself. And Samuel said to Saul, Why hast thou disquieted me, to bring me up...?"; "Moreover the LORD will also deliver Israel with thee into the hand of the Philistines: and to morrow shalt thou and thy sons be with me: and the LORD also shall

deliver the host of Israel into the hand of the Philistines." I Samuel 28:13-15a, 19

Does the sin of suicide erase your salvation from the LORD? After talking to a witch, the context illustrates that Samuel appeared in disgust to the witch and affirmed the future death of Saul and his destiny with Samuel. This truth was proved when Saul died. The sin of suicide did not alleviate Saul's security with the LORD!

> *"And when Ahithophel saw that his counsel was not followed, he saddled his ass, and arose, and gat him home to his house to his city, and put his household in order, and hanged himself, and died, and was buried in the sepulcher of this father." II Samuel 17:23*

It is ironic that many suicides follow this *"put his household in order"* mindset demonstrated in this verse.

DINOSAURS- The scripture speaks of dragons and large land/sea monsters.

> *"Behold now behemoth, which I make with thee: he eateth grass as an ox. Lo now, his strength is in his loins, and his force is in the navel of his belly. He moveth his tail like a cedar: the sinew of his stones are wrapped together. His bones are as strong pieces of brass; his bones are like bars of iron."*
> *"Canst thou draw out leviathan with an*

hook? Or his tongue with a cord which thou lettest down? Job 40:15-18; 41:1

DISMEMBERMENT-

> *"And when he was come into his house, he took a knife, and laid hold on his concubine, and divided her together with her bones, into twelve pieces, and sent her into all the coasts of Israel." Judges 19:29*

DRAFT- Twenty year old able bodied men were mandated for battle!

> *"Take ye the sum of all the congregation of the children of Israel, after their families, by the house of their fathers, with the number of their names, every male by their polls; From twenty years old and upward, all that are able to go forth to war in Israel: thou and Aaron shall number them by their armies." Numbers 1:2, 3*

> *"And Moses spake unto the people, saying, Arm some of yourselves unto the war, and let them go against the Midianites, and avenge the LORD of Midian. Of every tribe a thousand, throughout all the tribes of Israel, shall ye send to the war. So there were delivered out of the thousands of Israel a*

thousand of every tribe, twelve thousand armed for war." Numbers 31:3-5

DREAMS- The dictionary says that dreams are "a train of thought or images passing through the mind during sleep"[1]. Usually dreams are just plain weird, but these four examples show dreams as fearful, fleeting, full of folly and forward.

> *"Then thou scarest me with dreams, and terrifiest me through visions:" Job 7:14; "He shall fly away as a dream, and shall not be found: yea, he shall be chased away as vision of the night." Job 20:8; "It shall even be as when an hungry man dreameth, and behold, he eateth; but he awaketh, and his soul is empty: or as when a thirsty man dreameth, and, behold, he drinketh; but he awaketh, and behold, he is faint, and his soul hath appetite: so shall the multitude of all the nations be, that fight against mount Zion." Isaiah 29:8; "And if thou wilt walk in my ways, to keep my statutes and my commandments, as thy father David did walk, then I will lengthen thy days. And Solomon awoke; and, behold, it was a dream..." I Kings 3:14, 15*

Regardless of one's perception and without putting too much stock in the validity of dreams, we must be reminded to give the utmost value to the Word of God. The scriptures will stand alone for direction while dreams are inept because of uncertainty and confusion. Clarity will always be accomplished through the Son!

> *"GOD, who at sundry times and in divers manners spake in time past unto the fathers by the prophets, Hath in these last days spoken unto us by his Son, whom he hath appointed heir of all things, by whom also he made the worlds;" Hebrews 1:1, 2*

EMBALMING- Can you smell the spices?

> *"And Joseph commanded his servants the physicians to embalm his father: and the physicians embalmed Israel. And forty days were fulfilled for him; for so are fulfilled the days of those which are embalmed: and the Egyptians mourned for him three-score and ten days" Genesis 50:2, 3*

EMOTIONS-

BACKBITING- Have you ever heard "If you can't say anything good, then don't say anything at all"?

> *"LORD, who shall abide in thy tabernacle? Who shall dwell in thy holy hill? He that walketh uprightly, and worketh righteousness, and speaketh the truth in his heart. He that backbiteth not with his tongue, nor doeth evil to his neighbour, nor taketh up a reproach against his neighbour." Psalms 15:1-3; "Let*

no corrupt communication proceed out of your mouth, but that which is good to the use of edifying, that it may minister grace unto the hearers." Ephesians 4:29

BOASTING- No one is any better than anyone else. *"And these things, brethren, I have in a figure transferred to myself and to Apollos for your sakes; that ye might learn in us not to think of men above that which is written, that no one of you be puffed up for one against another. For who maketh thee to differ from another? And what hast thou that thou didst not receive? Now if thou didst receive it, why dost thou glory, as if thou hadst not received it? I Corinthians 4:6, 7*
"For by grace are ye saved through faith; and that not of yourselves: it is the gift of God: Not of works, lest any man should boast." Ephesians 2:9

ENVY-
"For we dare not make ourselves of the number, or compare ourselves with some that commend themselves: but they measuring themselves by themselves, and comparing themselves among themselves, are not wise." II Corinthians 10:12; "Let us not be desirous

of vain glory, provoking one another, envying one another." Galatians 5:26

FAVORITISM-
"These are the generations of Jacob. Joseph, being seventeen years old, was feeding the flock with his brethren: and the lad was with the sons of Bilhah, and with the sons of Zilpah, his father's wives: and Joseph brought unto his father their evil report. Now Israel loved Joseph more than all his children, because he was the son of his old age: and he made him a coat of many colours. And when his brethren saw that their father loved him more than all his brethren, they hated him, and could not speak peaceably unto him." Genesis 37:2-4; "I charge thee before God, and the Lord Jesus Christ, and the elect angels, that thou observe these things without preferring one before another, doing nothing by partiality." I Tim 5:21

HATES OF GOD- The odious attitude that permeates within these seven things is abominable.
"A proud look, a lying tongue, and hands that shed innocent blood, An heart that deviseth wicked imaginations, feet that be swift in running to mischief, A false witness that

speaketh lies, and he that soweth discord among brethren." Proverbs 6:17-19

INDIGNATION (RIGHTEOUS)- Do you ever get angry at sin?

"God judgeth the righteous, and God is angry with the wicked every day." Psalms 7:11; "And the Jews Passover was at hand, and Jesus went up to Jerusalem, And found in the temple those that sold oxen and sheep and doves, and the changers of money sitting: And when he had made a scourge of small cords, he drove them all out of the temple, and the sheep, and the oxen; and poured out the changers' money, and over threw the tables; And said unto them that sold doves, Take these things hence; make not my Father's house an house of merchandise." John 2:13-16

INDIGNATION (UNRIGHTIOUS) Do not empower an evil influence for the sake of being angry!

"Be ye angry, and sin not: let not the sun go down upon your wrath: Neither give place to the devil." Ephesians 4:26, 27

INSTABILITY-

"Confidence in an unfaithful man in time of trouble is like a broken tooth, and a foot out of joint." Proverbs 25:19; "A double minded mind is unstable in all his ways." James 1:8

INTEGRITY- So little of this exists today!

"Said he not unto me, She is my sister? And she, even she herself said, He is my brother: in the integrity of my heart and innocency of my hands have I done this. And God said unto him in a dream, Yea, I know that thou didst this in the integrity of thy heart; for I also withheld thee from sinning against me: therefore suffered I thee not to touch her." Genesis 20:5, 6; "Then said his wife unto him, dost thou still retain thine integrity? Curse God and die." Job 2:9; "The LORD shall judge the people: judge me, O LORD, according to my righteousness, and according to mine integrity that is in me." Psalms 7:8

JEALOUSY (POSITIVE)- We normally do not equate anything good to jealousy!

"For thou shalt worship no other god: for the LORD, whose name is Jealous, is a jealous God:" Exodus 34:14; "For I am jealous over you with godly jealousy: for I have espoused

you to one husband, that I may present you as a chaste virgin to Christ." II Corinthians 11:2

JEALOUSY (NEGATIVE)- This rarely turns out right.

"And the women answered one another as they played, and said, Saul hath slain his thousands, and David his ten thousands. And Saul was very wroth, and the saying displeased him; and he said, They have ascribed unto David ten thousands, and to me they have ascribed but thousands: and what can he have more but the kingdom? And Saul eyed David from that day and forward." I Samuel 18:7-9

LOVE- God himself not only defines but also describes charity!

"Beloved, let us love one another: for love is of God; and every one that loveth is born of God, and knoweth God. He that loveth not knoweth not God; for God is love. We love him, because he first loved us." I John 4:7, 8, 19; "Charity suffereth long, and is kind; charity envieth not ; charity vaunteth not itself, is not puffed up, Doth not behave itself unseemly, seeketh not her own, is not easily provoked, thinketh no evil;

Rejoiceth in the truth; Beareth all things, believeth all things, hopeth all things, endureth all things. Charity never faileth:..."
I Corinthians 13:4-8

LYING- Regardless of the reason we are all guilty.
"Wherefore putting away lying, speak every man truth with his neighbour: for we are members one of another. Ephesians 4:25; "But Peter said, Ananias, why hath Satan filled thine heart to lie to the Holy Ghost, and to keep back part of the price of the land?" Acts 5:3

VENGEANCE- Only danger lurks when self imposed.
"Dearly beloved, avenge not yourselves, but rather give place unto wrath: for it is written, Vengeance is mine saith the Lord." Romans 12:19; "Ye shall do no unrighteousness in judgment: thou shalt not respect the person of the poor, nor honour the person of the mighty: but in righteousness shalt thou judge thy neighbour." Leviticus 19:15; "Therefore Absalom sent for Joab, to have sent him to the king: but he would not come to him: and when he sent again the second time, he would not come. Therefore

he said unto his servants, See, Joab's field is near mine, and he hath barley there; go and set the field on fire." II Samuel 14:29, 30; "Not as Cain, who was of that wicked one, and slew his brother. And wherefore slew he him? Because his own works were evil, and his brother's righteous." I John 3:12

WRATH- Which side are you on?

"He that believeth on the Son hath everlasting life: and he that believeth not the Son shall not see life; but the wrath of God abideth on him." John 3:36; "For God hath not appointed us to wrath, but to obtain salvation

by our Lord Jesus Christ."
I Thessalonians 5:9

ENVIRONMENTAL PROTECTION AGENCY (EPA)- Although I am a proponent of protecting the environment, I know that the LORD never intended for the environment to dominate over man!

"And God said, Let us make man in our image, after our likeness: and let them have dominion over the fish of the sea, and over the fowl of the air, and over the cattle, and over all the earth, and over every creeping thing that creepeth upon the earth." Genesis 1:26

FASTING- The Bible varies in the length of abstaining from nourishment, but the acknowledgement and adoration toward the LORD should never vary!

> *"And I fell down before the LORD, as at the first, forty days and forty nights: I did neither eat bread nor drink water, because of all your sins which ye sinned, in doing wickedly in the sight of the LORD, to provoke him to anger."* Deuteronomy 9:18; *"Then all the children of Israel, and all the people, went up, and came unto the house of God, and wept, and sat there before the LORD, and fasted that day until even, and offered burnt-offerings and peace-offerings before the LORD."* Judges 20:26; *"Go, gather together all the Jews that are present in Shushan, and fast ye for me, and neither eat nor drink three days, night or day: I also and my maidens will fast likewise; and so will I go in unto the king, which is not according to the law: and if I perish, I perish."* Esther 4:16; *"And while the day was coming on, Paul besought them all to take meat, saying, This day is the fourteenth day that ye have tarried and continued fasting, having taken nothing."* Acts 27:33

FIRE WALKER- This is a hedonistic practice of idolatry.

"And thou shalt not let any of thy seed pass through the fire to Molech, neither shalt thou profane the name of thy God: I am the LORD" Leviticus 18:21, "But he walked in the way of the kings of Israel, yea, and made his son to pass through the fire, according to the abominations of the heathen, whom the LORD cast out from before the children of Israel." II Kings 16:3

FLIP FLOP- These scriptures demonstrate the difference between stability and instability.

"Of Zebulun, such as went forth to battle, expert in war, with all instruments of war, fifty thousand, which could keep rank: they were not of double heart." I Chronicles 12:33; "A double minded man is unstable in all his ways." James 1:8

GOVERNMENT- Judicial, Legislative and Executive

"For the LORD is our judge, the LORD is our lawgiver, the LORD is our king; he will save us." Isaiah 33:22; "Let every soul be subject unto the higher powers. For there is no power but of God: the powers that be are ordained of God." Romans 13:1

HEAVEN- JESUS references a place with the Father that has prepared mansions. He continues to prepare more mansions for those that will be in this place. He will return to receive those that have accepted His invitation and they will be with Him!

"In my Father's house are many mansions: if it were not so, I would have told you. I go to prepare a place for you. And if I go and prepare a place for you, I will come again, and receive you unto myself; that where I am, there ye may be also." John 14:2, 3

On the cross, JESUS told the malefactor where he would be after death.

"And Jesus said unto him, Verily I say unto thee, To day shalt thou be with me in paradise." Luke 23:43

"Paradise" is Heaven because JESUS is with the Father and the Father is in the third heaven.

"I knew a man in Christ above fourteen years ago, (whether in the body, I cannot tell; or whether out of the body, I cannot tell: God knoweth;) such an one caught up to the third heaven." II Corinthians 12:2

The space for the birds to fly is the first heaven and the celestial stars, planets, etc. reside in the second heaven.

"And God said, Let the waters bring forth abundantly the moving creature that hath life, and fowl that may fly above the earth in the

open firmament of heaven." Genesis 1:20;
"And God said, Let there be lights in the
firmament of the heaven to divide the day
from the night; and let them be for signs, and
for seasons, and for days, and years:"
Genesis 1:14

HELL- This is a biblical place that is the total opposite of
Heaven. Heaven is eternal life with the LORD and Hell is
eternal life without the LORD. An everlasting fire is the
destiny for the devil, his angels and everyone not found
written in the book of life.

> *"Then shall he say also unto them on the left*
> *hand, Depart from me, ye cursed, into*
> *everlasting fire, prepared for the devil and his*
> *angels:" Matthew 25:41. "And death and*
> *hell were cast into the lake of fire. This is the*
> *second death. And whosoever was not found*
> *written in the book of life was cast into the*
> *lake of fire." Revelation 20:14, 15*

Hell is also a place of torment where the worm does not die
nor the fire is quenched!

> *"And it came to pass, that the beggar died,*
> *and was carried by the angels in to*
> *Abraham's bosom: the rich man also died,*
> *and was buried: And in hell he lift up his eyes,*
> *being in torments, and seeth Abraham afar*
> *off, and Lazarus in his bosom. And he cried*

and said, Father Abraham, have mercy on me, and send Lazarus, that he may dip the tip of his finger in water, and cool my tongue: for I am tormented in this flame."
Luke 16:22-24

HUMAN SACRIFICE-

"Thou shalt not do so unto the LORD thy GOD: for every abomination to the LORD, which he hateth, have they done unto their gods; for even their sons and their daughters they have burnt in the fire to their gods."
Deuteronomy 12:31

LABOR UNIONS- Like minded people can produce a tumult!

"And the same time there arose no small stir about that way. For a certain man named Demetrius, a silversmith, which made silver shrines for Diana, brought no small gain unto the craftsmen: Whom he called together with the workmen of like occupation, and said, Sirs, ye know that by this craft we have our wealth. Moreover ye see and hear, that not alone at Ephesus, but almost throughout all Asia, this Paul hath persuaded and turned away much people, saying that they be no gods, which are made with hands: So that not only this our craft is in danger to be set at

nought; but also that the temple of the great goddess Diana should be despised, and her magnificence should be destroyed, whom all Asia and the world worshippeth. And when they heard these sayings, they were full of wrath, and cried out, saying, Great is Diana of the Ephesians." Acts 19:23-28

LIFE- The LORD is not only the giver of life, but He is also pro life. Life begins at conception and everyone is known by the LORD in the womb.

"Let the day perish wherein I was born, and the night in which it was said, There is a man child conceived." Because it shut not up the doors of my mother's womb, nor hid sorrow from mine eyes. Why died I not from the womb? Why did I not give up the ghost when I came out of the belly?" "I should have been as though I had not been; I should have been carried from the womb to the grave." Job 3:3, 10, 11; 10:19

Job is definitely speaking about life at conception. In this next verse we see that King David not only speaks about life at conception but also sin at conception!

"Behold, I was shapen in iniquity; and in sin did my mother conceive me." Psalm 51:5

Jeremiah is known in the womb before birth. It would be very difficult to have a plan for someone if he did not exist!

"Before I formed thee in the belly I knew thee; and before thou camest forth out of the womb I sanctified thee, and I ordained thee a prophet unto the nations." Jeremiah 1:5

Our physical existence is short and limited!

"For we are but of yesterday, and know nothing, because our days upon earth are a shadow" Job 8:9; "Go to now, ye that say, To day or to morrow we will go into such a city, and continue there a year, and buy and sell, and get gain: Whereas ye know not what shall be on the morrow. For what is your life? It is even a vapour, that appeareth for a little time, and then vanisheth away." James 4:13, 14

MUTILATION-

"And when he was come into his house, he took a knife, and laid hold on his concubine, and divided her, together with her bones, into twelve pieces, and sent her into all the coasts of Israel" Judges 19:29

RELIGIOUS APPEASEMENT

"And it came to pass at noon, that Elijah mocked them, and said, Cry aloud: for he is a

god; either he is talking, or he is pursuing, or he is in a journey, or peradventure he sleepeth, and must be awaked. And they cried aloud, and cut themselves after their manner with knives and lancets, till the blood gushed out upon them." I Kings 18:27, 28

NATURE- The LORD created nature, mother had nothing to do with it!

"He bindeth up the waters in his thick clouds: and the cloud is not rent under them."; "He hath compassed the waters with bounds, until the day and night come to an end." Job 26:8, 10; "The sun also ariseth, and the sun goeth down, and hasteth to his place where he arose. The wind goeth toward the south, and turneth about unto the north; it whirleth about continually, and the wind returneth again according to his circuits. All the rivers run into the sea; yet the sea is not full; unto the place from whence the rivers come, thither they return again." Ecclesiastes 1;5-7· "Thus saith the LORD, which giveth the sun for a light by day and the ordinances of the moon and of the stars for light by night, which divideth the sea when the waves thereof roar; The LORD of hosts is his name:" Jeremiah 31:35

NAVY-

> *"And king Solomon made a navy of ships in Ezion-geber, which is beside Eloth, on the shore of the Red sea, in the land of Edom. And Hiram sent in the navy his servants, shipmen that had knowledge of the sea, with the servants of Solomon." I Kings 9:26, 27*

PRIMPING-

COSMETICS- "Make-up" has been made up for many years!

> *"And when Jehu was come to Jezreel, Jezebel heard of it; and she painted her face, and tired her head, and looked out at a window." II Kings 9:30; "And when thou art spoiled, what wilt thou do? Though thou clothest thyself with crimson, though thou deckest thee with ornaments of gold, though thou rentest thy face with painting, in vain shalt thou make thyself fair; thy lovers will despise thee, they will seek thy life." Jeremiah 4:30; "And furthermore, that ye have sent for men to come from far, unto whom a messenger was sent; and, l, they came: for whom thou didst wash thyself, paintedst thy eyes, and deckedst thyself with ornaments," Ezekiel 23:40*

PERFUME- Sweet aromas and fragrances make statements.

"And Joab sent to Tekoah, and fetched thence a wise woman, and said unto her, I pray thee, feign thyself to be a mourner, and put on now mourning apparel, and anoint not thyself with oil, but be as a woman that had a long time mourned for the dead:" II Samuel 14:2; "Now when every maid's turn was come to go in to king Ahasuerus, after that she had been twelve months, according to the manner of the women, (for so were the days of their purifications accomplished, to wit, six months with oil of myrrh, and six months with sweet odours, and with other things for the purifying of the women;)" Esther 2:12

PRISONER SWAP- This is not an even swap. A murderer was chosen over the Saviour and the guilty was justified more than the innocent!

"And they had then a notable prisoner, called Barabbas. Therefore when they were gathered together, Pilate said unto them, Whom will ye that I release unto you? Barabbas, or Jesus which is called Christ? The governor answered and said unto them, Whether of the twain will ye that I release unto you? They said, Barabbas. Pilate saith unto them, What shall I do then with Jesus which is called Christ? They all say unto him, Let him be crucified. And the governor

said, Why, what evil hath he done? But they cried out the more, saying, Let him be crucified. Then released he Barabbas unto them, and when he had scourged Jesus, he delivered him to be crucified."
Matthew 27:16, 17, 21-23, 26

PULPIT- The Old Testament use of this word would be considered the preaching "platform" today. We utilize the term lectern for New Testament purposes!

"And Ezra the scribe stood upon a pulpit of wood, which they had made for the purpose..." Nehemiah 8:4

RAINBOW- A colored bow in the clouds is visible to us and also the LORD. The everlasting covenant between GOD and every living creature is remembered. A flood will never destroy the earth again.

"I do set my bow in the cloud, and it shall be for a token of a covenant between me and the earth. And it shall come to pass, when I bring a cloud over the earth, that the bow shall be seen in the cloud: And I will remember my covenant, which is between me and you and every living creature of all flesh; and the waters shall no more become a flood to destroy all flesh. And the bow shall be in the cloud; and I will look upon it, that I may remember the everlasting covenant between

God and every living creature of all flesh that is upon the earth." Genesis 9:13-16

SCORE- A Biblical measuring unit by twenties. Caleb lived beyond a good age!

> *"Forty years old was I when Moses the servant of the LORD sent me from Kadesh-barnea to espy out the land: and I brought him word again as it was in mine heart. And now, behold, the LORD hath kept me alive, as he said these forty and five years, even since the LORD spake this word unto Moses, while the children of Israel wandered in the wilderness: and now, lo, I am this day four-score and five years old." Joshua 14:7, 10; "The days of our years are threescore years and ten: and if by reason of strength they be fourscore years, yet is their strength labour and sorrow; for it is soon cut off, and we fly away." Psalm 90:10*

SEASONS

> *"While the earth remaineth, seedtime and harvest, and cold and heat, and summer and winter, and day and night shall not cease." Genesis 8:22; "He appointed the moon for seasons: the sun knoweth his going down." Psalm 104:19*

SEXUAL RELATIONS- Marriage between a man and woman is intimately blessed!

> *"Therefore shall a man leave his father and his mother, and shall cleave unto his wife: and they shall be one flesh. And they were both naked, the man and his wife, and were not ashamed." Genesis 2:24, 25; "Marriage is honourable in all, and the bed undefiled: but whoremongors and adulterers God will judge." Hebrews 13:4*

Any other relation is both perverse and an abomination!

ADULTERY-

"Thou shalt not commit adultery" Exodus 20:14

Even the lustful look is equal to the very act!

> *"Ye have heard that it was said by them of old time, Thou shalt not commit adultery: But I say unto you, That whosoever looketh on a woman to lust after her hath committed adultery with her already in his heart." Matthew 5:27, 28*

BEASTIALITY-

"Whosoever lieth with a beast shall surely be put to death." Exodus 22:19 "Neither shalt

thou lie with any beast to defile thyself therewith: neither shall any woman stand before a beast to lie down thereto: it is confusion." Leviticus 18:23

INCEST-
"It is reported commonly that there is fornication among you, and such fornication as is not so much as named among the Gentiles, that one should have his father's wife." 1 Corinthians 5:1

ORGY- Sexual wickedness wrongfully empowers credentials.
"And Ahithophel said unto Absalom, Go in unto thy father's concubines, which he hath left to keep the house; and all Israel shall hear that thou art abhorred of thy father: then shall the hands of all that are with thee be strong. So they spread Absalom a tent upon the top of the house; and Absalom went in unto his father's concubines in the sight of all Israel." II Samuel 16: 21, 22

PREMARITAL- Fornication is sex outside of marriage. Sleeping around or shacking up is wrong!
"And if a man entice a maid that is not betrothed, and lie with her, he shall surely

endow her to be his wife. If her father utterly refuse to give her unto him, he shall pay money according to the dowry of virgins."
Exodus 22:16, 17

PROSTITUTION-
"Do not prostitute thy daughter, to cause her to be a whore: lest the land fall to whoredom and the land become full of wickedness."
Leviticus 19:29

RAPE- This egregious lustful act is never good. Any sex outside of marriage is destructive. Men generally fulfill the well known cliché, "He just wants to get into your pants." After succeeding, disgust and disdain become prevalent and the man no longer pursues the woman. She will feel rejected and fear will induce silence. This is a terrible situation. The rapist should be exposed!
"And she answered him, Nay, my brother, do not force me; for no such thing ought to be done in Israel: do not thou this folly. And I, whither shall I cause my shame to go? and as for thee, thou shalt be as one of the fools in Israel. Now therefore, I pray thee, speak unto the king; for he will not withhold me from thee. Howbeit he would not hearken unto her voice: but, being stronger than she, forced

her, and lay with her. Then Amnon hated her exceedingly; so that the hatred wherewith he hated her was greater than the love wherewith he had loved her. And Amnon said unto her, Arise, be gone. And she said unto him, There is no cause: this evil in sending me away is greater than the other that thou didst unto me. But he would not hearken unto her. And Absalom her brother said unto her, Hath Amnon thy brother been with thee? But hold now thy peace, my sister: he is thy brother; regard, not this thing. So Tamar remained desolate in her brother Absalom's house." II Samuel 13:12-17, 20

GANG RAPE- Vile wickedness
"But the men would not hearken to him: so the man took his concubine, and brought her forth unto them; and they knew her, and abused her all the night until the morning: and when the day began to spring, they let her go." Judges 19:25

SODOMY- Homosexuality is a wicked abomination!
"But before they lay down, the men of the city, even the men of Sodom, compassed the house round, both old and young, all the people from every quarter: And they called

unto Lot, and said unto him, Where are the men which came in to thee this night? Bring them out unto us, that we may know them. And Lot went out at the door unto them, and shut the door after him. And said, I pray you, brethren, do not so wickedly." Genesis 19:4-7; "Thou shalt not lie with mankind, as with womankind: it is abomination." Leviticus 18:22; "If a man also lie with mankind, as he lieth with a woman, both of them have committed an abomination: they shall surely be put to death; their blood shall be upon them." Leviticus 20:13; "And likewise also the men, leaving the natural use of the woman, burned in their lust one toward another: men with men working that which is unseemly, and receiving in themselves that recompence of their error which was meet." Romans 1:27

Judgment rests with those that are an accomplice also!

"Who knowing the judgment of God, that they which commit such things are worthy of death, not only do the same, but have pleasure in them that do them." Romans 1:32

SIGNS OF AGING- No one wants to be a burden, but certain circumstances from an aging life can become a problem.   Thinking correctly and tasting and hearing well, are examples of physical ability without inhibition.

> *"I am this day fourscore years old: and can I discern between good and evil? Can thy servant taste what I eat or what I drink? Can I hear any more the voice of singing men and singing women? Wherefore then should thy servant be yet a burden unto my lord the king?   II Samuel 19:35*

SIMONY- The work of GOD is not for sale!

> *"And when Simon saw that through laying on of the apostles' hands the Holy Ghost was given, he offered them money, saying, give me also this power, that on whomsoever I lay hands, he may receive the Holy Ghost, but Peter said unto him, thy money perish with thee, because thou hast thought that the gift of God may be purchased with money."   Acts 8:18-20*

SPANKING- This is a biblical form of correction.

> *"Foolishness is bound in the heart of a child; but the rod of correction shall drive it far from him." Proverbs 22:15; "He that spareth his rod hateth his son: but he that loveth him chasteneth him betimes."   Proverbs 13:24; "Chasten thy son while there is hope, and let not thy soul spare for his crying."*

What's The Bible Got To Do With It?

Proverbs 19:18

SPIRITISM- Evil manifests itself through the spiritual world. God is a Spirit and any spiritual work outside of Him is an abomination. The following scriptures reveal a very real principle against looking toward or giving credit to divination, fortune tellers or speaking with the dead (necromancing)!

> *"Regard not them that have familiar spirits, neither seek after wizards, to be defiled by them: I am the LORD your God" Leviticus 19:31; "There shall not be found among you any one that maketh his son or his daughter to pass through the fire, or that useth divination, or an observer of times, or an enchanter, or a witch, or a charmer, or a consulter with familiar spirits, or a wizard, or a necromancer. For all that do these things are an abomination unto the LORD: and because of these abominations the LORD thy God doth drive them out form before thee." Deuteronomy 18:10-12; "And he caused his children to pass through the fire in the valley of the son of Hinnom: also he observed times, and used enchantments, and used witchcraft, and dealt with a familiar spirit, and with wizards: he wrought much evil in the sight of the LORD, to provoke him to anger." II Chronicles 33:6*

The spirits should be proved scripturally!
"Beloved, believe not every spirit, but try the spirits whether they are of God: because many false prophets are gone out into the world. Herby know ye the Spirit of God: Every spirit that confesseth that Jesus Christ is come in the flesh is of God: And every spirit that confesseth not that Jesus Christ is come in the flesh is not of God: and this is that spirit of antichrist, whereof ye have herd that it should come; and even now already is it in the world." I John 4:1-3

SPITTING- This is not just a nasty habit, but it is also a distasteful gesture! Spitting is used to show disdain.
"They abhor me, they flee far from me, and spare not to spit in my face." Job 30:10

Miriam, Moses' sister, is given leprosy for her rebellious action against authority. Even the LORD reveals the contempt for spitting as being put outside of social contact.
"And the cloud departed from off the tabernacle; and, behold, Miriam became leprous, white as snow: and Aaron looked upon Miriam, and, behold, she was leprous. And Moses cried unto the LORD, saying, Heal her now, O God, I beseech thee. And

the LORD said unto Moses, If her father had but spit in her face, should she not be ashamed seven days? Let her be shut out from the camp seven days, and after that let her be received in again."
Numbers 12:10, 13, 14

JESUS was despised and shown abhorrence.
"Then did they spit in his face, and buffeted him: and others smote him with palms of their hands.", "And they spit upon him, and took the reed, and smote him on the head."
Matthew 26:67, 27:30

David used his spittle to display a mental disorder.
"And David laid up these words in his heart, and was sore afraid of Achish the king of Gath. And he changed his behaviour before them, and feigned himself mad in their hands, and scrabbled on the doors of the gate, and let his spittle fall down upon his beard."
I Samuel 21:12, 13

On a positive note, JESUS used his own saliva and mixed it with clay to make an eye salve!
"When he had thus spoken, he spat on the ground, and made clay of the spittle, and he

anointed the eyes of the blind man with the clay." John 9:6

STRIPES- These beatings or whippings are a way to inflict judgment. The LORD JESUS CHRIST himself bore the penalty of our sin on His cross! We deserved the "stripes" but JESUS took them for us. In CHRIST, we are eternally and spiritually complete!

> *"But he was wounded for our transgressions, he was bruised for our iniquies: the chastisement of our peace was upon him; and with his stripes we are healed." Isaiah 53:5, "Who his own self bare our sins in his own body on the tree, that we, being dead to sins, should live unto righteousness: by whose stripes ye were healed." I Peter 2:24*

The apostle Paul suffered "stripes" for being in CHRIST JESUS!

> *"Are they ministers of Christ? (I speak as a fool) I am more: in labours more abundant, in stripes above measure, in prisons more frequent, in deaths oft. Of the Jews five times received I forty stripes save one." II Corinthians 11:23, 24*

The Old Testament records a judgment of "forty stripes" as a sufficient amount.

Anything above that would be considered abuse!

"And it shall be, if the wicked man be worthy to be beaten, that the judge shall cause him to lie down, and to be beaten before his face, according to his fault, by a certain number. Forty stripes he may give him, and not exceed: lest, if he should exceed, and beat him above these with many stripes, then thy brother should seem vile unto thee."
Deuteronomy 25:2, 3

No doubt this is where we get the cliché "Thirty-nine lashes!"

SWEAR- Swearing is never good. It is better to "swear" not! Swear words reveal a verbal ignorance and diminished vocabulary instead of communicating intelligently!

"Thou shalt not take the name of the LORD thy God in vain; for the LORD will not hold him guiltless that taketh his name in vain."
Exodus 20:7, "And ye shall not swear by my name falsely, neither shalt thou profane the name of thy God: I am the LORD."
Leviticus 19:12

Most everyone knows that taking the "LORD's" name in vain is wrong but, too often, slang is used instead. "Gosh darn" and

"O my God" are standard responses! The latter is especially egregious because "God" is referenced in an ungodly way and the guilty person rarely knows "God" personally!

"But I say unto you, Swear not at all: neither by heaven; for it is God's throne: Nor by the earth; for it is his footstool: neither by Jerusalem; for it is the city of the great King. Neither shalt thou swear by thy head, because thou canst not make one hair white or black. But let your communication be, Yea, yea: Nay, nay: for whatsoever is more than these cometh of evil." Matthew 5:34-37, "But above all things, my brethren, swear not, neither by heaven, neither by the earth, neither by any other oath: but let your yea be yea; and your nay, nay; lest ye fall into condemnation." James 5:12

How much more clear, concise communication does one need?

TREASURES- Almost always described as financial gain however, instead of gold, silver, precious metals or some other monetary value, the Bible recognizes an unfamiliar depository!

"Hast thou entered into the treasures of the snow? Or hast thou seen the treasures of the hail." Job 38:22, "He causeth the vapours to ascend from the ends of the earth; he maketh

lightnings for the rain; he bringeth the wind out of his treasuries." Psalm 135:7

TRINITY- God the Father, God the Son, God the Holy Spirit is equally one! Each was present in creation and each is necessary for conversion. God the Father planned our salvation, God the Son provided our salvation and God the Holy Spirit pleads to all their need for salvation! Although the word "trinity" is not in the Bible, the wonderful truth is! The word "us" is always more than one.

> *"And God said, Let us make man in our image, after our likeness: and let them have dominion over the fish of the sea, and over the fowl of the air, and over the cattle, and over all the earth, and over every creeping thing that creepeth upon the earth." Genesis 1:26, "For there are three that bear record in heaven, the Father, the Word, and the Holy Ghost: and these three are one." I John 5:7*

VOWS- Promises are made many times without any desire to keep but, a vow is a serious matter and it should be kept!

> *"If a man vow a vow unto the LORD, or swear an oath to bind his soul with a bond; he shall not break his word, he shall do according to all that proceedeth out of his mouth." Numbers 30:2, "When thou vowest a vow unto God, defer not to pay it; for he hath no pleasure in fools: pay that which thou hast*

vowed. Better is it that thou shouldest not vow, than that thou shouldest vow and not pay." Ecclesiastes 5:4, 5

WHIRLWIND- A Heaven bound Tornado!
"And it came to pass, as they still went on, and talked, that, behold, there appeared a chariot of fire, and horses of fire, and parted them both asunder; and Elijah went up by a whirlwind into heaven." II Kings 2:11

WINDING STAIRS- These have been around a long time.
"The door for the middle chamber was in the right side of the house: and they went up with winding stairs into the middle chamber, and out of the middle into the third." I Kings 6:8

WOMANHOOD- Whatever state a woman is in can be praise worthy!
"He maketh the barren woman to keep house, and to be a joyful mother of children. Praise ye the LORD." Psalms 113:9

BARREN WOMB- To be childless may be perceived as a reproach.
"And God remembered Rachel, and God hearkened to her, and opened her womb. And she conceived, and bare a son; and said, God hath taken away my reproach:" Genesis

30:22, 23, "But unto Hannah he gave a worth portion; for he loved Hannah: but the LORD had shut up her womb. And her adversary also provoked her sore, for to make her fret, because the LORD had shut up her womb." I Samuel 1:5, 6

Let's be reminded that Hannah did have a son, named Samuel.

"And she said, Let thine handmade find grace in thy sight. So the woman went her way, and did eat, and her countenance was no more sad. And they rose up in the morning early, and worshiped before the Lord, and returned, and came to their house to Ramah; and Elkanah knew Hannah, his wife; and the Lord remembered her. Wherefore it came to pass, when the time was come about after Hannah had conceived, that she bear a son, and called his name Samuel, saying, Because I have asked him of the Lord." I Samuel 1:18-20

BREAST FEEDING- This is a God given natural and biblical blessing to nourish children. Sarah was able past ninety years old!

"And she said, Who would have said unto Abraham, that Sarah should have given

children suck? for I have born him a son in his old age." Genesis 21:7, "but thou art he that took me out of the womb: thou didst make me hope when I was upon my mother's breasts." Psalms 22:9, "Gather the people, sanctify the congregation, assemble the elders gather the children, and those that suck the breasts:" Joel 2:16

HELP MEET- The husband's wife is never before him or behind him but, always on his side. She completes him!
"And the LORD God said, it is not good that the man should be alone: I will make him an help meet for him." Genesis 2:18

KEEPER OF HOME- The woman definitely makes a house a home!

"That they may teach the young women to be sober, to love their husbands, to love their children, to be discreet, chaste, keepers of home, good, obedient to their own husbands, that the word of God be not blasphemed." Titus 2;4, 5

MENSTRUATION-
"Now Abraham and Sarah were old and well stricken in age: and it ceased to be with Sarah

after the manner of women."; "And she said to her father, let it not displease my lord that I cannot rise up before thee; for the custom of women is upon me. And he searched, but found not the images." Genesis 18:11, 31:35

VIRGINITY- The most important virgin is Mary the mother of JESUS! With her virginity, we have a promised and provided sinless Saviour!
"Therefore the LORD himself shall give you a sign; behold, a virgin shall conceive, and bear a son, and shall call his name Immanuel." Isaiah 7:14, "Behold, a virgin shall be with child, and shall bring forth a son, and they shall call his name Emmanuel, which being interpreted is, God with us." Matthew 1:23

Scripturally, a virgin should remain a virgin until marriage. Outside of marriage, when she is no longer a virgin, she should marry!
"There is difference also between a wife and a virgin. The unmarried woman careth for the things of the Lord, that she may be holy both in body and in spirit: but she that is married careth for the things of the world, how she may please her husband. But if any man think that he behaveth himself uncomely

toward his virgin, if she pass the flower of her age, and need so require, let him do what he will, he sinneth not: let them marry."
I Corinthians 7:34, 36

What's The Bible Got To Do With It?

FAITH

Although mostly unknown, faith is one of the greatest gifts known to man. Scriptural faith is in the LORD JESUS CHRIST! Throughout life we are led to believe that religion and faith are synonymous, but the two words do not mean the same thing! In Second Peter chapter one and verse one we are given a profound verse.

> *"Simon Peter, a servant and an apostle of Jesus Christ to them that have obtained like precious faith with us through the righteousness of God and our Saviour Jesus Christ."*

Peter is not generalizing faith to be multifaceted, but he is pinpointing faith to a specific person. The classic statements "we all have faith in someone" or "I have one faith and you have another faith" still remains unbiblical. Because faith (reliance, fidelity) is in the person of Jesus Christ, then anyone or anything else will not suffice for a biblical saving faith. We can put our trust or belief in many things, but I am a solifidian in the Lord Jesus Christ. He wholly and solely is our hope for eternal life in heaven. The following "faith" verses are laid out to enlighten, equip and encourage the saints to yield a stronger faith every day.

"For ye are all the children of God by faith in Christ Jesus"[1] because *"even the righteousness of God which is by faith of Jesus Christ unto all and upon all them that believe: for there is no difference."*[2] We are *"testifying both to the Jews, and also to the Greeks, repentance toward God, and faith toward our Lord Jesus Christ."*[3] *"Therefore being justified by faith, we have peace with God through our Lord Jesus Christ"*[4] and *"that your faith should not stand in the wisdom of men, but in the power of God."*[5] We remember *"that from a child thou hast known the holy scriptures, which are able to make thee wise unto salvation through faith which is in Christ Jesus."*[6] *"For by grace are ye saved through faith: and that not of yourselves: it is the gift of God: not of works, lest any man should boast."*[7] *"Now faith is the substance of things hoped for, the evidence of things not seen"*[8] *"but without faith it is impossible to please him: for he that cometh to God must believe that he is, and that he is a rewarder of them that diligently seek him."*[9] *"For therein is the righteousness*

of God revealed from faith to faith: as it is written, the just shall live by faith."[10]

"For we walk by faith, not by sight"[11] and *"knowing this, that the trying of your faith worketh patience"*[12] so *"that the trial of your faith, being much more precious than of gold that perisheth, though it be tried with fire, might be found unto praise and honour and glory at the appearing of Jesus Christ."*[13] Never forget *"that ye should earnestly contend for the faith which was once delivered unto the saints."*[14] *"Let no man despise thy youth; but be thou an example of the believers, in word, in conversation, in charity, in spirit, in faith, in purity"*[15]*"so that we ourselves glory in you in the churches of God for your patience and faith in all your persecutions and tribulations that ye endure."*[16]

"Examine yourselves, whether ye be in the faith; prove your own selves. Know ye not your own selves, how that Jesus Christ is in you, except ye be reprobates?"[17] *"For whatsoever is born of God overcometh the world: and this is the victory that overcometh the world, even our faith."*[18] With this, *"the disciples said unto the Lord, increase our faith."*[19]

What's The Bible Got To Do With It?

"As we have therefore opportunity, let us do good unto all men, especially unto them who are of the household of faith"[20] and *"above all, taking the shield of faith, wherewith ye shall be able to quench all the fiery darts of the wicked."[21]* *"Knowing that a man is not justified by the works of the law, but by the faith of Jesus Christ, even we have believed in Jesus Christ, that we might be justified by the faith of Christ, and not by the works of the law: for by the works of the law shall no flesh be justified."[22]* *"Only let your conversation be as it becometh the gospel of Christ: that whether I come and see you, or else be absent, I may hear of your affairs, that ye stand fast in one spirit, with one mind striving together for the faith of the gospel."[23]*

So *"that Christ may dwell in your hearts by faith; that ye, being rooted and grounded in love."[24]* *"For though I be absent in the flesh, yet am I with you in the spirit, joying and beholding your order, and the steadfastness of your faith in Christ."[25]* We are *"remembering without ceasing your work of faith, and labour of love, and patience of hope in our Lord Jesus Christ, in the sight of God and our Father."[26]* *"Yea, and if I be offered upon the sacrifice and service of your faith, I joy, and rejoice with you all."[27]* *"For from you sounded out the word of the Lord not only in Macedonia and Achaia, but also in every place your faith to God-ward is spread abroad; so that we need not to speak anything."[28]*

Inside this soliloquy of scriptures resides the faithful testimony of the Word of God! We can live day by day being conformed to these verses. Knowing how to be saved is one thing, but living out that faith requires an eighteen inch (head to heart) decision. Years ago, I came to the reality that I was lost. In my mind, I knew about JESUS CHRIST, but I had never believed in Him for salvation. From my heart, I believed by faith. You will never be spiritually saved until you admit that you are spiritually lost!

Because faith is in the person of JESUS CHRIST, these faith verses are useful for daily life. The Bible tells us to walk by faith and not by sight (II Cor 5:7). The reality of trials and tribulations are a constant reminder for our need of guidance. When the Lord allows challenges to strengthen us, we know that applying these "faith" verses will bring victory after each trial and tribulation! Are you provoked to ask the same apostle request?

"And the apostles said unto the Lord, Increase our faith" Luke 17:5

Many try to use self-examination to prove (test) their faith through personal accomplishments, but scripturally, we know that our faith is rooted in the Lord and made perfect through His grace. It is impossible to perfect ourselves through our own ability or merit. When you stop trying to hold up or hold on to yourself, then a precious faith for a perfect rest is received. The world needs to know that true faith in the LORD JESUS CHRIST is the only faith that gives man total satisfaction and complete rest!

1. Galatians 3:26

2. Romans 3:22

3. Acts 20:21

4. Romans 5:1

5. I Corinthians 2:5

6. II Timothy 3:15

7. Ephesians 2:8, 9

8. Hebrews 11:1

9. Hebrews 11:6

10. Romans 1:17

11. II Corinthians 5:7

12. James 1:3

13. I Peter 1:7

14. Jude 3

15. I Timothy 4:12

16. II Thessalonians 1:4

17. II Corinthians 13:5

18. I John 5:4

19. Luke 17:5

20. Galatians 6:10

21. Ephesians 6:16

22. Galatians 2:16

23. Philippians 1:27

24. Ephesians 3:17

25. Colossians 2:5

26. I Thessalonians 1:3

27. Philippians 2:17

28. II Thessalonians 1:8

What's The Bible Got To Do With It?

FAMILY

Wow, I find myself overwhelmed with such gratitude as I write this chapter! The Bible has plenty to say about the family. The family includes the home, marriage, husband, wife and children. Let us realize that the LORD started the family and He has given instructions for each facet of the family.

My early years encompassed an alcoholic dad, a broken home and divorced parents. This caused me to understand and know what does not work. Those formidable years were hard lessons but, they did propel me to an understanding of what does work. Not until I got born again did I learn to apply biblical truths to develop a GOD honoring family! Quickly, because of biblical proverbs and other passages, I found out that the Word of God works! The biblical principles written throughout the scriptures will teach and produce a family that is pleasing to the Lord. The Bible is not a one, two, three instruction book for bringing up a family but, it does relate examples to follow, mistakes that were made and counsel to be received. I am very thankful that the Lord never makes humanity palatable or superficially attractive. He portrays sin as sin and wise choices as wise choices.

Is it possible to actually formulate guidelines from the Word of God to make a family work? Granted, it would seemingly be easier if a chapter or one book in the Bible was specifically dedicated to the family. Since individual people in individual families have unique situations and circumstances, it would be difficult to make all families a "one size fits all". Honestly, uniformity would be boring! Throughout the Bible, truths, principles and applications are given to guide a family that will be pleasing to the Lord. Certainly within the Bible, we see good and bad choices that were made and knowing what not to do or learning from others mistakes are just as conducive as the positive lessons.

The Lord has given us the family. A man and woman were created to procreate children in order to produce a godly heritage. Unfortunately, we live in a dysfunctional society and the "traditional" family structure is no longer valued. Now, anything outside the normal is considered normal and we are supposed to understand and accept it. The Bible is no stranger to dysfunctional families. The classic dysfunctional example is in the life of Jacob (Genesis 29-31; 34-37). A man with four wives and thirteen children was impaired by some dysfunctional moments. He had some unity but also strife, animosity and favoritism.

Without a doubt, whether good or bad decisions, we must learn from others' benefits and or mistakes. We can learn something from Jacob's family because they did not always see eye to eye with one another. Intrigue, love, jealousy, hate and envy were a few emotions that Jacob's family experienced. Each family has their moments but in the end it should be their heritage that keeps them together. It bothers me when families do not get along. My mom had three miscarriages and three other children that lived. One of those three lived past two and he, the only brother that I knew, died at sixteen in a car accident. Since age nineteen, I have been an only child and honestly when I see siblings fight or lack communication it just does not sit well with me.

As my wife, Tammy, and I began our family, I wanted to stress togetherness and family time. I always loved meeting as a family for meals and enjoyed the children's conversation. There is something about being around the table communicating with the kids that really blessed me! Having five children in seven and a half years was interesting and exciting. They grew up close and they are all still very close in their relationships. By the way, the teenage years to me were the best.

So, where has the Bible helped me? If God created the family, and He did, then we can follow and trust His instructions. My broken family upbringing was not a positive influence for raising our family but, through that experience, I desired to change our family's outcome for the positive. In Genesis we read about the home that started with Adam and Eve. I for one am glad that the Lord said it was not good for Adam to be alone.

"And the Lord God said, it is not good that the man should be alone; I will make him an help meet for him... And the rib, which the

LORD God had taken from man, made he a woman, and brought her unto the man... Therefore shall a man leave his father and his mother, and shall cleave unto his wife; and they shall be one flesh" Genesis 2:18, 22, 24

God created Eve from Adam's rib and they began their companionship with one another. The woman completed the man and the strength of two became one. As unto the LORD, the only family member that you have the privilege to choose is your spouse. Choose wisely!

"Whoso findeth a wife findeth a good thing, and obtaineth favour of the Lord" Proverbs 18:22

Since 1985, I have thankfully enjoyed *"a good thing"*. I am learning to dwell with my wife for friendship and togetherness while we walk side by side. I love the co-existence with my wife. There is a special comfort in marriage that speaks without words and enjoys a loving glance from across the room. Tammy and I had an equal determination to go in the same direction. Certainly Joshua chapter twenty four and verse fifteen has a special and encouraging place in our marriage.

"And if it seem evil unto you to serve the Lord, choose you this day whom ye will serve whether the gods which your fathers served that were on the other side of the flood, or the gods of the Amorites, in whose land ye dwell:

but as for me and my house, we will serve the Lord"   Joshua 24:15

Even though Tammy was raised with a totally different environment than I was, we both needed to make the choice ourselves. My need for faster knowledge to apply truth was much greater than for my wife. Our admiration for the Lord began a wonderful journey to seek the Lord in prayer and Bible study. Yes, a husband and wife have different areas to excel within the family but, working together with an attitude for success allows for rest in the Lord as He builds a family for His glory!

How fast can everything you have sought after and built up be torn down? Very fast! The scriptures reveal a truth in the Book of Judges chapter two.

"And also all that generation were gathered unto their fathers: and there arose another generation after them, which knew not the Lord, nor yet the works which he had done for Israel. And the children of Israel did evil in the sight of the Lord, and served Baalim: And they forsook the Lord god of their fathers, which brought them out of the land of Egypt and followed other gods, of the gods of the people that were round about them, and bowed themselves unto them, and provoked the Lord to anger. And they forsook the Lord and served Baal and Ashtaroth."
Judges 2.10-13

What's The Bible Got To Do With It?

In one generation everything can change. Although the deterioration has been going on for some time in our society, I didn't want to be a statistic. It seems that the generational breakdown is in full force but, my heart is to nurture the next generation so that they will know and serve the LORD. We desired that our children would not just hear about how to walk with the LORD but see it also. Not just hear about the works of the LORD but to see and experience the power of God in their lives. Our kids knew that serving the LORD was what we did. It is too prevalent today for parents to send their children to church and not attend themselves. As Tammy and I served the LORD, our children were with us every step of the way. What will become of the next generation? Remember that the "other gods" are still around but they can never save or deliver. This question will be answered soon enough but, as for our family, we desired to break the chain of non-existent Christ likeness in order to start a heritage of Christ likeness.

As for our family, Tammy and I, we want to experience all the possible joy that the marriage has to offer. God writes about many beautiful relationships between a husband and a wife. Isaac and Rebekah, Jacob and Rachel, Boaz and Ruth come to mind just to name a few. I can honestly say that we have been given a godly, biblical, devoted love. I certainly like sporting with my wife!

"And it came to pass, when he had been there a long time, that Abimelech king of the Philistines looked out at a window, and saw,

and, behold, Isaac was sporting with Rebekah his wife". Genesis 26:8

First Corinthians chapter thirteen promotes love as an action word and Song of Solomon portrays the unquenchable and endearing love between two that are devoted to one another as unto the Lord. Too often in marriage, couples dwell on the negative instead of the positive. We all have our faults and pet peeves but, the special opportunity to see beyond the human idiosyncrasies is to our advantage.

"Forbearing one another, and forgiving one another, if any man have a quarrel against any: even as Christ forgave you, so also do ye." Colossians 3:13

As the years go by, we are reminded of the joy of a love that overlooks and out performs. One thing is for sure, there is a real and necessary need to commit and submit to one another. With that in mind, the classic scriptural passage is found in the Book of Ephesians chapter five.

"Submitting yourselves one to another in the fear of God. Wives, submit yourselves unto your own husbands, as unto the Lord. For the husband is the head of the wife, even as Christ is the head of the church: and he is the Saviour of the body. Therefore as the church is subject unto Christ, so let the wives be to their own husbands in everything. Husbands, love your wives, even as Christ also loved the

church, and gave himself for it;"
Ephesians 5:21-25

Profound truth is found in verse twenty one. Each person in the marriage is responsible to submit to one another under their God given role. If the husband will be the husband and the wife will be the wife, then the marriage will be blessed and blissful.

To think that, according to the scriptures, the marriage relationship is our picture of the relationship between Christ Jesus and His church is very humbling. No greater expression of love can be portrayed in the world. Christ Jesus does love the church. He did give His life for her. The church is subject to Christ Jesus as the head. The false understanding about domination or blind submission is unfortunate. The husband has his role and the wife has hers. Neither should cross each other but both should edify one another. Neither the husband nor the wife has the right to discount or belittle the other. If the husband or the wife speaks contrary to each other, then in return they have spoken contrary to themselves. Nothing bothers me more than to listen to husbands or wives speak negatively or make a joke about their spouse. We are so thankful to have upheld one another with encouraging and edifying words. To my knowledge we have never spoken against one another. What people think they can gain with contrary words is really a loss to me and a sad outcome for their marriage. Does it make sense that the church speak contrary against the "head" or vice versa? I think not! So much the more do we see the significance and necessity of marital commitment!

Many books have been written about man's need for respect and the woman's need for security. Just knowing this need will not produce the desired outcome. The old adage of fifty percent for both sides is wrong. We must give one hundred percent on both sides. Both the husband and wife are responsible to be under the Lord's authority. A relationship has two sides and both must be involved for the relationship to thrive. Selfishness is sin but submission is sweet. Each role has a responsibility to be unified spiritually and physically.

> *"Therefore shall a man leave his father and his mother, and shall cleave unto his wife: and they shall be one flesh." Genesis 2:24*

As the years go by, Tammy and I are closer now than when we were first married. Spending time with one another is crucial. Each year of our marriage, we have tried to go away together at least twice for a couple of days without the kids. You learn how to not abuse nor misuse one another! Being "one flesh" is a great biblical principle. The Bible allows for the marriage to enjoy endless possibilities. Is it possible to have a marriage that is beyond your expectation? We think so and we want to respond actively on purpose! We even express that we are still on our honeymoon; not bad after all these years!

> *"Only by pride cometh contention: but with the well advised is wisdom" Proverbs 13:10*

We both desire to nourish and cherish our marriage. Our communication is vital and learning how to speak to one another is very important. This verse has made a tremendous difference in understanding why contention exists and how to respond with caution. Pride becomes a wedge in any relationship and all involved need to understand that it has divisive power. When someone does not get treated right or expects a different reaction to a situation, etc.; we know that feelings can get hurt or stepped on. Regardless of how a disagreement begins, this verse reminds us that pride is contentious and never the solution.

"Except the Lord build the house, they labour
in vain that build it..." Psalms 127:1

We believe that in every family experience there is a heavenly purpose. The heavenly example of Christ and His church should be lived out within an earthly marriage. We have the designer and the plans for a successful home. The Builder has blessed us with five awesome children and that responsibility has made us mindful of who is really in control! From the beginning, we gave our children to the Lord to do with them as He sees fit. Why would anyone want to diminish the opportunity to have anything less than all that the Lord can accomplish?

The Book of Deuteronomy chapter six speaks about a great principle for the family.

"That thou mightest fear the Lord thy God, to
keep all his statutes and his commandments,
which I command thee, thou, and thy son, and

thy son's son, all the days of thy life; and that
thy days may be prolonged. Hear therefore,
O Israel, and observe to do it; that it may be
well with thee, and that ye may increase
mightily, as the Lord God of thy fathers hath
promised thee, in the land that floweth with
milk and honey." Deuteronomy 6:2, 3

These verses speak volumes and ring loudly about a heritage and the continued promised blessings. As mentioned before, on my side of the family, I wanted to break the chain of non-Christ likeness and begin a heritage of Christ likeness. Malachi chapter two and verse fifteen is another verse that testifies a heritage through a *"godly seed."*

"Lo, children are an heritage of the Lord:
and the fruit of the womb is his reward."
Psalms 127:3

Has the depth of a Godly heritage penetrated sufficiently yet? Children are a blessing but they belong to the Lord.

"And these words, which I command thee this
day, shall be in thine heart: And thou shalt
teach them diligently unto thy children, and
shalt talk of them when thou sittest in thine
house, and when thou walkest by the way, and
when thou liest down, and when thou risest
up. And thou shalt bind them for a sign upon
thine hand, and they shall be as frontlets

between thine eyes. And thou shalt write them upon the posts of thy house, and on thy gates." Deuteronomy 6:6-9

These verses exemplify the necessity for real parental attributes and that "the parents" are responsible to distinctly enact them. Children are very attentive and they can detect hypocrisy. They will observe sincerity that is both spoken and lived out. True biblical faith that is taught will be transmitted from the parents. Our desire was to teach with an interest to know more and grow deeper in biblical knowledge. It is very difficult to teach something that you do not know. I understand that not all children will completely apply everything that they are taught. Some will even reject with rebellion but, we have no excuse to slack in our responsibility because, as parents, we will give an account one day. These verses encompass an all-around complete life to teaching our children. If we separate ourselves or leave off areas of parenthood, our children will assume their own boundaries!

"The rod and reproof give wisdom: but a child left to himself bringeth his mother to shame." Proverbs 29:15

Insistence and repetition are very necessary and the best way for teachable moments in life is talking, sitting, walking, lying down and rising up! Spending quality time with the children should never get old. Being genuinely involved in their lives is paramount. We tried to always have an open mind and an inclined ear for conversation.

Authentic interest, insistence, and involvement will be perceived as real and biblical principles.[1] Many excuses can be given but living godly truths will bring godly blessings!

We will talk about training and discipline later but, it is clear that children are on loan to us from the Lord and that each husband and wife in their respective families is responsible to know the Lord and to make Him known. We should strive to make this a reality first and foremost in the family!

LADIES- Wives/Moms have an awesome God given role as help meet, companion and care taker.

> *Likewise, ye wives, be in subjection to your own husbands; that, if any obey not the word, they also may without the word be won by the conversation of the wives; While they behold your chaste conversation coupled with fear. Whose adorning let it not be that outward adorning of plaiting the hair, and of wearing of gold, or of putting on of apparel; But let it be the hidden man of the heart, in that which is not corruptible, even the ornament of a meek and quiet spirit, which is in the sight of god of great price. For after this manner in the old time the holy women also, who trusted in God, adorned themselves, being in subjection unto their own husbands:"*
> *I Peter 3:1-5*

Because the previous chapter gives precedence to CHRIST's example, wives are encouraged to be guided by the same principles. Being a godly woman that will understand her position will easily promote submission. Subjecting herself to JESUS CHRIST will yield the greatest benefit to her husband. The wives conversation will not just be heard but it will also be seen. Her dedication to detail without question will be known by her husband. Obviously, her inward beauty should never be squelched. Too many women adorn the outward appearance with gaudy decoration and never let the inward person be adorned. When you meet one, a true godly lady is exemplary and carries herself with distinct class!

I want to express a gift that I gave my wife. I heard that the greatest gift a dad could give his children was to love their mom. I love my wife and I love my wife in front of our children. Seriously, it is easy to love her because Tammy is an example of a Proverbs chapter thirty one woman. The submitted and not belittled wife lives within a tremendous blessing. My wife has lived to fulfill her responsibilities and has not tried to be the man. She has a voice and is vital in decisions but the brunt of the final outcome belongs to the man. I understand that too many men will not uphold their part of the family but, that does not give the woman a right to be both the mom and the dad. I believe that if a man will lead then his wife will follow. Any other deviation from that order will become problematic.

> *"She looketh well to the ways of her household, and eateth not the bread of idleness. Her children arise up, and call her*

blessed; her husband also, and he praiseth her." Proverbs 31:27, 28

Because the way of the household resides with the woman, I believe she should give all diligence to that outcome. This will be praise worthy from her children and her husband. Moreover, the husband will be better known and esteemed blessed because of his wife.

"Her husband is known in the gates, when he sitteth among the elders of the land." Proverbs 31:23

Her ministry as keeper of home is paramount in many ways. Moms give nurture and comfort during the formidable children years.

"That they may teach the young women to be sober, to love their husbands, to love their children, to be discreet, chaste, keepers at home, good, obedient to their own husbands, that the word of God be not blasphemed." Titus 2:4, 5

Without apology, mothers should exemplify affection and should be pure and not lewd, innocent and not brash and should endear their God given position with temperance and modesty! Have you ever heard that "There are many women but not many ladies?" Too many children are left to raise themselves and our society today reveals this dilemma. My wife counted the cost and esteemed the responsibility "keeper at home" to be a blessing. One of my favorite quotes from my wife is that she is a "domestic engineer". Is there a more truthful statement? Certainly, a house wife is not cursed but she is very blessed. She has the great privilege to see her children grow up and to influence them for the Lord. Moms' skills are manifested in many ways as a wise shopper, diligent seamstress, strong, sincere and steady to continue throughout her day.

When is a mother's work ever done? The answer is never! While children are home there will always be something to do. My wife has received this as a blessing. Mindful to be thankful for even the dishes and clothes to wash! Bearing children is one thing but bearing fruit from those children is quite another thing.

> *"Thy wife shall be as a fruitful vine by the sides of thine house: thy children like olive plants roundabout they table." Psalms 128:3*

I believe this is where my wife gets the phrase *"bloom where you are planted"*. Labor is assured to bring children in to this world but, much labor is needed to bring up children. Hannah in the Book of First Samuel prayed to the Lord to be given a child for him.

> *"And she vowed a vow, and said, O Lord of hosts, if thou wilt indeed look on the affliction of thine handmaid, and remember me, and not forget thine handmaid, but wilt give unto thine handmaid a man child, then I will give him unto the Lord all the days of his life, and*

there shall no razor come upon his head. For this child I prayed; and the Lord hath given me my petition which I asked him: Therefore also I have lent him to the Lord; as long as he liveth he shall be lent to the Lord. And he worshipped the Lord there." I Samuel 1:11, 27, 28

The great prophet Samuel was the result of her prayer and Hannah followed through with her promise! No one is guaranteed children but the responsibility to raise children is profound. Women, wives, moms are vital in the family that the Lord has made. Without them the existence of any of us would be impossible. Even our Lord Jesus Christ utilized a woman's womb through a virgin born birth!

Obviously, you can't start a family without a mom. Years ago I read a beautiful story that pictures how great, astute, busy and blessed moms are. This will put a smile on your face.

Why I Love Mom

Mom and Dad were watching TV when Mom said, I'm tired, and it's getting late I think I'll go to bed. She went to the kitchen to make sandwiches for the next day's lunches. Rinsed out the popcorn bowls, took meat out of the freezer for supper the following evening, checked the cereal box levels, filled the sugar container, put spoons and bowls on the table and started the coffee pot for brewing the next morning. She then put some wet clothes in the dryer, put a load of clothes into the washer, ironed a shirt and secured a loose button. She picked up the game pieces left on the table, put the phone back on the charger and put the telephone book into the drawer. She watered the plants, emptied a wastebasket and hung up a towel to dry. She yawned and stretched and headed for the bedroom. She stopped by the desk and wrote a note to the teacher, counted out some cash for the field trip, and pulled a textbook out from hiding under the chair. She signed a birthday card for a friend, addressed and stamped the envelope and wrote a quick note for the grocery store. She put both near her purse. Mom then washed her face with 3 and 1 cleanser, put on her night solution and age fighting moisturizer, brushed and flossed her teeth and filed her nails. Dad called out, "I thought you were going to bed." I'm on my way, she said. She put some water in to the dog's dish and put the cat outside, then made sure the doors were locked and the patio light was on. She looked in on each of the kids and turned out their bedside lamps and tv's, hung up a shirt, threw some dirty socks into the hamper, and had a brief conversation with one up still doing homework. In her own room, she set the alarm; laid out clothing for the next day, straightened up the shoe rack. She added three things to her six most important things to do list. She said her prayers and visualized the accomplishments of her goals. About that time, Dad turned off the TV and announced to no one in particular "I'm going to bed." And he did... without another thought. (Author Unknown)

Wives and moms should be more appreciated and thanked. Thank you Ladies!

MEN- Husbands/Dads have a huge responsibility. Without taking anything lightly, I have been blessed to be both a husband and a dad. I believe that I will speak with more authority about the man because I am the male part of the marriage. The Lord has given the man the brunt of the responsibility within the marriage. Let me say that the woman can either make or break the outcome of the man but, in the end, he is responsible for his family.

The battle for the family to remain relevant is at epic proportions. It is not by chance that without a strong male voice, the historical traditional family will be unheard of. No longer does popular sitcoms such as "Father Knows Best", My Three Sons", "Leave it to Beaver", "Little House on the Prairie" and "The Cosby Show" mold the mind of society. Rather, "Married with Children", "The Simpson's", "Family Guy" and "South Park" denigrate the elevated position of man to buffoonery and mockery. The traditional family is ridiculed and even commercials portray the male as stupid or lacking sensibility for family decisions.

Is it any wonder why Satan subtly arrived in the Garden of Eden to oppose the LORD's plan?

> *"Now the serpent was more subtil than any beast of the field which the LORD God had made. And he said unto the woman, Yea, hath God said, Ye shall not eat of every tree of the garden? And the woman said unto the serpent, We may eat of the fruit of the trees of the garden: But of the fruit of the tree which is in the midst of the garden, God hath said, Ye shall not eat of it, neither shall ye touch it, lest ye die. And the serpent said unto the woman, Ye shall not surely die: For God doth know that in the day ye eat thereof, then your eyes shall be opened, and ye shall be as gods, knowing good and evil. And when the woman saw that the tree was good for food, and that it was pleasant to the eyes, and a tree to be desired to make one wise, she took of the fruit thereof, and did eat, and gave also unto her husband with her: and he did eat. And the eyes of them both were opened, and they knew that they were naked; and they sewed fig leaves together, and made themselves aprons." Genesis 3:1-7*

Through verbal deception, Eve was tricked and Satan's subtle deceit won over Adam. It is no surprise that Satan's onslaught went through the woman to get to the man. Men are such pushovers when it comes to women. Sin beguiled man and spiritual death began.

> *"Wherefore, as by one man sin entered into the world, and death by sin; and so death passed upon all men, for that all have sinned:"* Romans 5:12

How important is the man in the home? GOD gave Adam the instructions and he thwarted his responsibilities and negated to share truth with his wife.

> *"And the LORD GOD took the man, and put him into the Garden of Eden to dress it and to keep it. And the LORD GOD commanded the man, saying, Of every tree of the garden thou mayest freely eat: But of the tree of the knowledge of good and evil, thou shalt not eat of it: for in the day that thou eatest thereof thou shalt surely die."* Genesis 2:15-17

This cunning devious plan to destroy the family is not new but, it is a totally twisted, purposeful, satanic design to dismantle GOD's created family. Satan wants to ruin the family because he knows that the man is the stalwart of the greatest institution along with the Church of JESUS CHRIST! Men are accountable to the LORD and He gives us an awesome privilege to esteem the family with the highest regard.

As for being a husband, mannerisms should be given great consideration.

> *"Likewise, ye husbands, dwell with them according to knowledge, giving honour unto the wife, as unto the weaker vessel, and as being heirs together of the grace of life; that your prayers be not hindered."*
> *I Peter 3:7*

Physical- *"dwell with them"*. If the night out with the boys is more important than spending time with your wife, your marriage will be second best. Although career and provision is paramount, far too often the wives get the leftovers. The wife deserves the husband's undivided attention and sincere communication that looks her straight in the eye. Intellectual- *"according to knowledge"*. How well do married couples really know one another? When dating began you had a crush but, why is communication now a bunch of mush? The only way to grow in knowledge is to learn from one another. Is it possible that your love will grow deeper as your knowledge of one another is greater? It is no surprise to me that this verse is directed to the husband. I am still learning how to communicate with better purpose and intent!

Emotional- *"giving honour unto the wife"*. High credentials are given to the wife. She is to be handled lovingly and with much care. As a fine piece of precious crystal (weaker vessel) would never be mishandled, neither should a wife. Esteeming one another during marriage is just as important as before marriage. Husbands/wives should never take one another for granted.

Spiritual- *"that your prayers be not hindered"*. How well the husband adjusts to the first part of this verse will speak volumes about his prayer life. No husband in his right mind would desire to have his prayers hindered. Otherwise, what value is it to have a prayer life? A hindered prayer will cut to the heart of a heartfelt prayer. When his example is honoring to the LORD, his marriage will be in great condition.[2]

As for the family man, the Lord relates a profound principle with Abraham in Genesis 18:17-19

> *"And the LORD said, Shall I hide from Abraham that thing which I do: Seeing that Abraham shall surely become a great and mighty nation, and all the nations of the earth shall be blessed in him? For I know him, that he will command his children and his household after him, and they shall keep the way of the LORD, to do justice and judgment, that the LORD may bring upon Abraham that which he hath spoken of him."*

We are told that the Lord knows Abraham and that he will have his household (wife & children) in order and they will follow him. His household shall keep the way of the Lord and do justice and judgment. I see the reality of integrity in this example because Abraham would do what is right and correct what is wrong. The Lord did not speak or make this known to everybody but unto Abraham only. The primary responsibility belongs to the head of the household. The Lord has thoughts toward the man of the home that are special and, in obedience, the blessings will be known. Although the Lord did not force Abraham to obey Him, the Lord knew that the heart of Abraham would choose the right way.

> *"And God said unto Jacob, Arise, go up to Beth-el, and dwell there: and make there an altar unto God that appeared unto thee when thou fleddest from the face of Esau thy brother. Then Jacob said unto his household, and to all that were with him, Put away the strange gods that are among you, and be clean, and change your garments: And let us arise, and go up to Beth-el: and I will make there an altar unto God, who answered me in the day of my distress, and was with me in the way which I went. And they gave unto Jacob all the strange gods which were in their hand, and all their earrings which were in their ears; and Jacob hid them under the oak which was by Shechem. And they journeyed; and the terror of God was upon the cities that were round about them, and they did not pursue after the sons of Jacob."*
> *Genesis 35:1-5*

Abraham's grandson, Jacob, receives a profound principle for family restoration. He was to return to Beth-el (the house of God) in order to be restored. We are in a great restoration need for the family today. The kingdom of this world has very strong influential tactics. These influences will distract and deceive to bring disarray to the family structure. Jacob was told to be pure, unadulterated, uncontaminated and to cast out the worldly influences. Under the authority of God, Jacob knew that he needed to be back where he could communicate and receive an answer from the Lord! Once again, we see that Jacob, the leader, received this truth and not the other individual family members.

Although I previously mentioned Psalms 127, I want to elaborate further.

> *"Except the LORD build the house, they labour in vain that build it: except the LORD keep the city, the watchman waketh but in vain. It is vain for you to rise up early, to sit up late, to eat the bread of sorrows: for so he giveth his beloved sleep. Lo, children are an heritage of the LORD: and the fruit of the womb is his reward. As arrows are in the hand of a mighty man; so are children of the youth. Happy is the man that hath his quiver full of them; they shall not be ashamed, but they shall speak with the enemies in the gate."*
> *Psalms 127:1-5*

We can watch out for the outcome but, if the Lord is not first, than our "watch" is in vain. Our work, preoccupation or worry, is vain and sleep will be inhibited if the Lord is not preeminent. The Lord is the giver of children and He will reward His heritage. If the reward is merited, than our desire will be to have children that grow up and produce a godly heritage after us. Arrows in the hand of the mighty man is mentioned. Like arrows, children should be strong, straight and set in order. Surely an archer has his arrows with the fletching and tips well-kept and ready to hit the mark. When the Lord is preeminent, our sleep will be sweet and the family voice will reveal unashamed fullness!

"And, ye fathers, provoke not your children to wrath: but bring them up in the nurture and admonition of the LORD." Ephesians 6:4

This verse should captivate every father's attention. Without provocation, the Bible gives the father the ability to nurture children with the right example and to admonish them with the right teaching. These exhortations are huge responsibilities that provoke the father to take correct aim when raising children. An archer will have the most correct and conditioned arrows to be at his best and the father will certainly desire to have his children directed to be the most effective. Then Psalm 127:5 says *"happy is the man"* that has his progeny unashamed and a heritage that will speak unabashed with the adversaries. This Psalm has really helped me in my journey of raising children. In reality, the home belongs to the LORD and He will produce a heritage for His glory! Yes, it is true that a man can be happy that has his quiver full. These truths from the Word of God have given me much reason to pray and also great joy to read, study, and apply them.

Abraham and Isaac are a classic dad and son relationship example. Of course, in Genesis twenty two we see a direct dad and son correlation between our Heavenly Father and Heavenly Son!

> *"And it came to pass after these things, that God did tempt Abraham and said unto him, Abraham: and he said, Behold, here I am. And he said, Take now thy son, thine only son Isaac, whom thou lovest, and get thee into the land of Moriah: and offer him there for a burnt-offering upon one of the mountains which I will tell thee of. And Abraham rose up early in the morning, and saddled his ass, and took two of his young men with him, and Isaac his son, and clave the wood for the burnt-offering, and rose up, and went unto the place of which God had told him. Then on the third day Abraham lifted up his eyes, and saw the place afar off. And Abraham said unto his young men, abide ye here with the ass; and I and the lad will go yonder and worship, and come again to you. And Abraham took the wood of the burnt-offering, and laid it upon Isaac his son; and he took the fire in his hand,*

and a knife; and they both of them together. And Isaac spake unto Abraham his father, and said, my father: and he said, here am I, my son. And he said, behold the fire and the wood: but where is the lamb for a burnt-offering? And Abraham said, my son, God will provide himself a lamb for a burnt-offering: so they went both of them together. And they came to the place which God had told him of: and Abraham built an altar there, and laid the wood in order, and bound Isaac his son, and laid him on the altar upon the wood. And Abraham stretched forth his hand, and took the knife to slay his son. And the angel of the LORD called unto him out of heaven, and said, Abraham, Abraham: and he said, Here am I. And he said, lay not thine hand upon the lad, neither do thou anything unto him: for now I know that thou fearest God, seeing thou hast not withheld thy son, thine only from me. And Abraham lifted up his eyes, and looked, and behold behind him a ram caught in a thicket by his horns: and Abraham went and took the ram, and offered him up for a burnt-offering in the stead of his son. And Abraham called the name of that place Jehovah-jireh: as it is said to this day, in the mount of the LORD it shall be seen."
Genesis 22:1-14

Worshipping with your children is a great privilege. In this chapter Abraham and Isaac went away together to worship. They spent time together and obviously this had not been a new thing because there was nothing unusual about their journey. Abraham was to spend spiritual time with his promised son whom he loved. Abraham knew that regardless of the outcome he would return from worship with his son. Is there any greater promise than that? The LORD promised Abraham that He would make a great nation through him in Genesis twelve. With that promise in mind, Abraham was confident that even though the purpose of their journey was to sacrifice his son Isaac; they would return from worshipping together. When you worship the LORD with your children, you can be assured that the outcome will be good!

This passage tells us that Abraham and Isaac not only worshipped together but they also worked together. Although both Abraham and Isaac carried some altar material, Isaac knew that the lamb was missing. Isaac's altar building experience prompted the question about the lamb.

I always enjoyed working around the house and teaching the kids to work together. Being in the ministry, we were able to include our children in many activities. Like Abraham and Isaac, we were able to establish a visible work ethic. It certainly is better to show a work ethic than to speak about one. Abraham and Isaac were both willing to accomplish the end result. Nothing was withheld for the sacrifice because Abraham was willing to offer his son and

Isaac was willing to be offered. Total obedience was the key and the LORD did provide himself as a sacrificial lamb for the sacrifice.

Why is it that we hold back? Dads, we have everything at our disposal and we are without excuse because of the scriptures. It is the LORD that makes us a dad and who also gives us children. We have no right to withhold anything that we are called to do. Children are a temporary assignment and I desire the multiplied blessing that Abraham received. Words alone will not rise up a godly heritage but deeds are also needed!

> *"And whatsoever ye do in word or deed, do all in the name of the LORD JESUS, giving thanks to God and Father by him."*
> *Colossians 3:17*

This powerful truth challenged me to be real and live before our children consistently. Whether in worship, at work, or wherever I am, may my life and communication say "what you see is what you get" no matter what to the glory of God!

Kelle Hein

A FATHER'S ABC's

*A*lways trust your children to God's care
*B*ring them to church
*C*hallenge them to high goals
*D*elight in their achievements
*E*xalt the LORD in their presence
*F*rown on evil
*G*ive them love
*H*ear their problems
*I*gnore not their childish fears
*J*oyfully accept their apologies
*K*eep their confidence
*L*ive a good example before them
*M*ake them your friends
*N*ever ignore their endless questions
*O*pen your heart to their love
*P*ray for them by name
*Q*uicken your interest in their spirituality
*R*emember their needs
*S*how them the way of salvation
*T*each them to work
*U*nderstand they are still young
*V*erify your statements
*W*ean them from bad company
*X*pect them to obey
*Y*earn for God's best for them
*Z*ealously guide them in Bible truth
Author-Unknown

What's The Bible Got To Do With It?

Now, Dads and Moms, it is time for the children!
Years ago while standing inside the Buffalo Bill Historical
Center in Cody, Wyoming, I watched a dad and his son
walking toward the door. With a discourse of words and
waving of hands, they entered the building and the dad said
to me "Kids, you got to love em' you can't shoot em".
Having five kids of my own, I honestly laughed and
understood his frustration while receiving his jest. At times,
raising children has its moments but, what a blessing they
are. Sometimes it is hard to remember that we, the parents,
were once children ourselves.

Whether or not you have had a biblical upbringing,
the Bible should be your guide to cherish along the way.

"Train up a child in the way he should go:
and when he is old, he will not depart from
it." Proverbs 22:6

Raising children is definitely not for wimps. My disciplined
approach to teaching by example is not merely a show.
Children can see through a façade and trickery. When true
learning is real, we rejoice in the promise that as children get
older their training will be applied. Even so much the more
do us as parents need to know biblically "how" the child
should go! Yes, the formidable years are a temporary
assignment however; parents have the awesome
responsibility to prepare their children to live in the world.

"But continue thou in the things which thou
hast learned and hast been assured of,
knowing of whom thou hast learned them;

And that from a child thou hast known the holy scriptures, which are able to make thee wise unto salvation through faith which is in Christ Jesus. All scripture is given by inspiration of God, and is profitable for doctrine, for reproof, for correction, for instruction I righteousness:"
II Timothy 3:14-16

The apostle Paul challenged young Timothy to continue in what he was taught. In the first letter to Timothy we are told that he had a godly mom and grandmother. Paul reminded Timothy to let their influence and teaching be applied to his life each day. The scriptures were used to train up and the necessary wisdom followed. What better training manual exists for profitable wisdom? Enclosed in the above verses, we understand that doctrine is what is right, reproof is what is wrong, correction is how to get right, and instruction is how to stay right. I certainly would have liked to have been equipped with this wisdom in my formidable years.

We have all been in a store listening to or watching a rebellious child throw a fit while screaming profusely. The incessant child usually under the duress of the mother, gets his/her way. Your inner thought screams 'take that kid out and spank em". Painstakingly, your stare ends in disgust as you walk away.

What's The Bible Got To Do With It?

"He that spareth his rod hateth his son: but he that loveth him chasteneth him betimes"
Proverbs 13:24

This verse helped me to train our children in two ways. The first is a tool and the second is timing. A rod is a tool that is very useful and without a rod my love will be lacking. I realize that abuse is a concern and too much correction is done in anger but, the Bible reveals effectiveness with a rod. This rod can be a stick or scion better known to most as "the switch".

"Foolishness is bound in the heart of a child; but the rod of correction shall drive it far from him." Proverbs 22:15

Can the usefulness of the rod be more precisely derived than from this verse?

"He that spareth his rod hateth his son: but he that loveth him chasteneth him betimes." Proverbs 13:24

Timing, that is to say early, is not only crucial but also pertinent. Betimes is a word that hastens chastening. "Before it is too late" is a cliché that may well serve parents in raising children. If the child controls the home at three years old, then you can pretty much be assured that problems will occur at thirteen years old. To love is to correct and to allow a child to grow up without boundaries is to equate hate!

"Chasten thy son while there is hope, and let not thy soul spare for his crying."
Proverbs 19:18

This verse reminds me about two stories when our children were very young. We had three in diapers at one time and a lady came up to me and said "You know it gets harder, later on, don't you?" I responded by saying "You have got to be kidding me." I am here to tell you that she was wrong because the scripture is my hope. The time that you put in raising children when they are three, four, and five will give you great hope when they are thirteen, fourteen, and fifteen. The other time was when our boys were young and they talked back to their grandma. At that moment, I looked up some proverbs and made a plan. I proceeded to bluntly proclaim that by the grace of God their back talk would stop. Cry and whine, throw a fit, do as you want but remember that correction will be the consequence to your decision. I am quite thankful that from that time on, back talk was not tolerated.

> *"For whom the Lord loveth he chasteneth, and scourgeth every son whom he receiveth. If ye endue chastening, God dealeth with you as with sons; for what son is he whom the father chasteneth not? But if ye be without chastisement, whereof all are partakers, then are ye bastards, and not sons. Furthermore we have had fathers of our flesh which corrected us, and we gave them reverence:*

shall we not much rather be in subjection unto the Father of spirits, and live? For they verily for a few days chastened us after their own pleasure; but he for our profit, that we might be partakers of his holiness. Now no chastening for the present seemeth to be joyous, but grievous: nevertheless afterward it yeildeth the peaceable fruit of righteousness unto them which are exercised thereby."
Hebrews 12:6-11

This passage is a classic teaching for raising children. In light of my responsibility, I will certainly correct my children because I love them! Although I would love to correct other children, I hesitantly refrain. Chastening or correcting our God given children is not an option to reject. It does not take a village to raise a family but, a dad and mom under the authority of the LORD! The LORD chastens us for our profit because an end result is at stake. His holiness will bring joy and fruitfulness. We always explained to our children the reason for the necessary spanking or tough communication. They always knew the reason for responsive correction to their consequential choices. Some of our children needed some little correction and some needed a LITTLE more. Verse eleven substantiates that the fruit of righteousness is produced through chastened exercise. Our children sometimes had selective forgetfulness and they received the necessary corrective exercise. When the pain and hurt subsided, a joyous and peaceful obedience ensued.

> *"The rod and reproof give wisdom: but a child left to himself bringeth his mother to shame. Correct thy son, and he shall give thee rest; yea, he shall give delight unto thy soul." Proverbs 29:15, 17*

With a rod as your tool and reproof in the right time, a mother will be unashamed. Our Creator never mandated the children to rule the household. It is a delight to have been blessed with children and I am so thankful that my wife, Tammy, and I have been given the responsibility to raise five children.

What's The Bible Got To Do With It?

FINANCE

Money is not the root of all evil but the "love" of money is. First Timothy chapter six is quite explicit concerning the uncertainty and deception of money. Proverbs twenty three and verse five portrays that money flies and Ecclesiastes chapter five verse twelve labors the fact that worrying about money will steal your sleep.

So, what is the big deal? It is still just money, right? Will you be able to take it with you after this life on earth? Of course not! However, the Bible says that we are *"pilgrims on the earth" (Hebrews 11:13)*, just passing thru but, why then are we collecting so much stuff to stay?

BASE-

> *"Charge them that are rich in this world, that they be not high minded, nor trust in uncertain riches, but in the living God, who giveth us richly all things to enjoy: That they do good, that they be rich in good works, ready to distribute, willing to communicate; Laying up in store for themselves a good foundation against the time to come, that they may lay hold on eternal life."*
> *I Timothy 6:17-19*

Money can play tricks with the mind and destroy the true meaning of trust. Too many enrich themselves in the pursuit of money but rarely are satisfied when they have it. The true purpose of life concerning money matters is to utilize riches for others to reap the personal benefit that God lovingly records.

> *"Moreover the profit of the earth is for all: the king himself is served by the field. He that loveth silver shall not be satisfied with silver; nor he that loveth abundance with increase: this is also vanity. When goods increase, they are increased that eat them: and what good is there to the owners thereof, saying the beholding of them with their eyes? The sleep of a labouring man is sweet, whether he eat little or much: but the abundance of the rich will not suffer him to sleep. There is a sore evil which I have seen under the sun, namely, riches kept for the owners thereof to their hurt. But those riches perish by evil travail: and he begetteth a son, and there is nothing in his hand. As he came forth of his mother's womb, naked shall he return to go as he came, and shall take nothing of his labour, which he may carry away in his hand. And this also is a sore evil, that in all points as he came, so shall he go: and what profit hath he*

that   hath   laboured   for   the   wind?
Ecclesiastes 5:9-16

This is a powerful revealing truth concerning the deceitfulness of riches. Because riches are a gift from God to enjoy, wealth should not be unappreciated. The Lord designed for everyone to enjoy earth's spoils but He never intended for one person to own them all. The desire for affluence will only promote dependence on the need to have more and cause sleep deprivation. Affluence breeds danger because it draws more people to the spoil and deceives the eye sight. Affluence, as well as life, can disappear quickly and nothing will be left to show in the end.[1]

BUSINESS
Even with the pit falls, money is still necessary. Our world is centered on filthy lucre and the Bible necessitates the use of money.

> *"And he called his ten servants, and delivered*
> *them ten pounds, and said unto them, Occupy*
> *till I come." Luke 19:13*

This verse is a direct correlation to being good stewards. Verse thirteen precedes a passage which concentrates around production. The word "occupy" is an interesting word, used only one time in the New Testament, which measures wise business practices. "Occupy", means to busy oneself with work or deeds in business matters. The servants were given financial gifts to invest for profit; however, the results were quite different. Even if one does not obey this principle, putting money in the bank for interest is better than nothing. We are all busy in life but the business of life should be for the one to whom everything belongs! Nothing really belongs to us.

A man named Job from the Old Testament exposes the truth about this subject.

> *"And said, Naked came I out of my mother's womb, and naked shall I return thither: the LORD gave, and the LORD hath taken away; blessed be the name of the LORD." Job 1:21*

Under much duress, Job reveals an accounting principle after losing his financial and family wealth. Life is too short to be self-centered and one does not have to own much to be selfish. All of us have attitudes or motives when it comes to finances but, where does it all end? If selfishness is our motive than we will never understand the awesome principle that it is better to give than to receive.

> *"I have shewed you all things, how that so labouring ye ought to support the weak, and to remember the words of the LORD JESUS, how he said, It is more blessed to give than to receive." Acts 20:35*

If the end results for planning and working are your kids or grandkids, then what? Is this really the end motive and do we still have a good attitude about it? Too often family members argue and fight over an inheritance that the deceased earned. When we are gone and our descendants enjoy the benefits of our hard work, will those finances be used, misused, or abused? Instead of trusting someone else to spend your money wisely, I believe the wiser choice is to be an individual steward and "occupy" for the glory of the LORD!

BREAKDOWN-

> *"But thou shalt remember the LORD thy God: for it is he that giveth thee power to get wealth, that he may establish his covenant which he sware unto thy fathers, as it is this day." Deuteronomy 8:18*

Because this is true, then there should not be any problem with wealth, right? Obviously, there is a problem! Who is really in control, money or man? Although we want to see the positives of financial freedom, we know the negative aspects still exist. The truth of Proverbs thirty verses eight and nine speaks of an attitude in the midst of two financial extremes.

> *"Remove far from me vanity and lies: give me neither poverty nor riches; feed me with food convenient for me: Lest I be full, and deny thee, and say, who is the LORD? Or lest I be poor, and steal, and take the name of my God in vain." Proverbs 30:8, 9*

Either poverty or riches can affect us in drastic ways. It is hard to imagine wanting poverty but we will take our chances with riches. Poverty is one thing but we all think that we can handle riches. When we think everyone else is not as spiritual or smart as we are, we realize that example after example continues to prove the failure of the classic human statement "it will not happen to me"!

> *"And a certain ruler asked him, saying, Good Master, what shall I do to inherit eternal life? And Jesus said unto him, Why callest thou me good? None is good, save one, that is, God. Thou knowest the commandments, Do not commit adultery, do not kill, Do not steal, Do not bear false witness, Honour thy father and thy mother. And he said, All these have I kept from my youth up. Now when Jesus heard these things, he said unto him, Yet lackest thou one thing: sell all that thou hast, and distribute unto the poor, and thou shalt have treasure in heaven: and come, follow me. And when he heard this, he was very sorrowful: for he was very rich. And when Jesus saw that he was sorrowful, he said, How hardly shall they that have riches enter into the kingdom of God!"*
> *Luke 18:18-24*

The ruler that asked the most important question to JESUS was bound by his supposed obedience but, selfishness overshadowed his bartering tool. The ruler proclaimed the longevity of his knowledge and obedience but, JESUS challenged him about his motive behind the proclamation. True treasure in heaven is in obedience from the heart. No matter how great sorrow can affect your demeanor, the deceitfulness of riches is greater!

Without a doubt, nobody knows when their life will end. The rich man in Luke Chapter twelve is not called a fool for nothing.

"And he spake a parable unto them, saying, The ground of a certain rich man brought forth plentifully: And he thought within himself, saying, What shall I do, because I have no room where to bestow my fruits? And he said, This will I do: I will pull down my barns, and build greater; and there will I bestow all my fruits and my goods. And I will say to my soul, Soul, thou hast much goods laid up for many years; take thine ease, eat, drink, and be merry. But God said unto him Thou fool, this night thy soul shall be required of thee: then whose shall those things be, which thou hast provided? So is he that layeth up treasure for himself, and is not rich toward God." Luke 12:16-21

What's The Bible Got To Do With It?

The farmers harvest was plentiful but his eternal planning was pathetic. The farmer had some covetous accounting with a carefree attitude. Prosperity became his propensity to be self-centered and not God centered. The possessions were not heaven's treasures but hoarded treasures. True riches will be laid up for us in a heavenly bank account when our possessions work for the eternal and not temporal!

Over the years many stories of misallocated funds have surfaced. Neither business nor church financial accounts have been denied these stories. When anyone thinks that everyone else's money belongs to them, greed lurks near. There will never be a shortage of dangerous, thieving charlatans.

> *"Then took Mary a pound of ointment of spikenard, very costly, and anointed the feet of Jesus, and wiped his feet with her hair: and the house was filled with the odour of the ointment. Then saith one of his disciples, Judas Iscariot, Simon's son, which should betray him, why was not this ointment sold for three hundred pence, and given to the poor? This he said, not that he cared for the poor; but because he was a thief, and had the bag, and bare what was put therein. Then said Jesus, Let her alone: against the day of my burying hath she kept this."* John 12:3-7

Concerning the treasury, we find a classic example of greed, selfishness and covetousness in the life of Judas Iscariot. Although the other disciples were in agreement against Mary, we find Judas castigating Mary for her "waste" of an expensive ointment. JESUS, on the other hand, was very pleased with her. When a thief holds the bag, one can expect a fleshly response but, when a spiritual reason is in play, honesty and integrity will be exemplified!

The ruler, the farmer, and Judas reveal strong examples that greed, selfishness and covetousness are never good. Each attitude and motive was a detriment to the favor of wealth. Because of these negative attributes, the financial blessings were broken down. Money can take you many directions but the final depository is the true test.

BUILDING-

"Lay not up for yourselves treasures upon earth, where moth and rust doth corrupt, and where thieves break through and steal: but lay up for yourselves treasures in heaven, where neither moth nor rust doth corrupt, and where thieves do not break through nor steal: for where your treasure is, there will your heart be also." Matthew 6:19-21

In my humble opinion this is the greatest incentive for financial giving in the entire world because the benefits are out of this world! There is not a better safe than in heaven Heavenly treasures are securely kept and can be neither robbed nor destroyed. Giving for an eternal outcome will always produce a greater dividend.

Many benevolence opportunities and giving to charities exist but, although each is very meritorious, will they advance the Kingdom of God solely on their own?

> *"He that hath a bountiful eye shall be blessed; for he giveth of his bread to the poor" Proverbs 22:9*

This verse confirms that anyone wanting to be a blessing will be blessed because he gives to the poor. However, without an avenue for the gospel to be preached, even feeding the poor will only be a temporary fix! The LORD JESUS himself substantiates the impoverished duration of society.

> *"For ye have the poor always with you; but me ye have not always." Matthew 26:11*

Where is our heart? We put great value and a high price on many things that are nothing but temporal. The moth and rust eat well but why not feed the eternal? It is the LORD JESUS CHRIST himself that tells us to lay up, put up, and store up treasures in heaven! If our only motive is to acquire riches in order to acquire more riches, then what will be in our heavenly account?

Ministries that will help the helpless, bless the beleaguered, and feed the poor while giving the gospel are proven ways and means to build treasures in heaven. The greatest entity to give into and give out from is the local New Testament Church. I am a proponent of giving toward opportunities that I know will be directly used toward winning the souls of men. The use of food, medicine, clothes, buildings and etc. are all awesome tools in order to preach, teach, and reach an eternal destiny. If our efforts bless the earthly, so much the more should we not bless the heavenly?

When is the right time to lay up for yourselves treasures in heaven? I believe the Bible teaches that now is the time. Too many are building themselves an earthly kingdom instead of building the "Kingdom of Heaven". If not now, when? Let us heed the Bible and utilize our monetary interests toward the heavenly. Our ability and opportunity to make wise fiscal sense is a fleeting entity. I say again, now is the time, while we have the time.

During the Civil War, a man with a large amount of money in gold coins lived near Murfreesboro, Tennessee. When Union forces entered the area in 1862, he was afraid they would take his money, so he buried it in a field near his farm. He made notes of the exact location of the treasure using trees and rocks as markers. During the melee, the occupying Union soldiers cut down the trees for firewood and gathered rocks to form chimneys for their barracks and fire pits. When the war ended, the man returned; but everything was different, and he was unable to locate his fortune. He spent the rest of his life trying to find the lost coins.[2]

Too many people are burying their riches in this life. Things change, health depletes, and life ends, etc. My mom always used to say "Do not put off to tomorrow what you can do today". We all know that we may never have the opportunity later. All fear aside, we do not have to worry because when we give to the LORD, our investments are secure!

The Grace of God will lead you toward eternal giving. Grace giving is a principle that is taught in the New Testament.

> *"Therefore as ye abound in everything, in faith, and utterance, and knowledge, and in all diligence, and in your love to us, see that ye abound in this grace also."*
> *II Corinthians 8:7*

Much has been written about this truth and I am thankful to have a part. The Missionary Apostle Paul received a financial gift from the Churches of Macedonia. Paul exhorted the Corinthian Church to abound in this grace giving also. Of course, giving of ourselves is the first prerequisite to giving however; we should prepare and plan to give our possessions for a greater cause beyond ourselves.

> *"And this they did, not as we hoped, but first gave their own selves to the LORD, and unto us by the will of God."* *II Corinthians 8:5*

Tithing or ten percent is a biblical measure of giving and it has also been used to quantify a religious obligation. Grace giving has never been or ever will be an obligation. Seriously, grace giving is beyond the tithe. When it comes to giving, most people do not even give a tithe and too many give grudgingly instead of cheerfully.

> *"Every man according as he purposeth in his heart, so let him give; not grudgingly, or of necessity: for God loveth a cheerful giver."*
> *II Corinthians 9:7*

How wonderful it is to purposefully give from the heart! This heartfelt desire is not moved by expectation or duty but by gratitude and a good attitude. The tithe is just a place to start the measurement. It is not even a prayer request. Does it not sound ridiculous to ask the LORD, should I give my tithe? Grace giving is more, beyond, in addition to your ten percent. Giving by grace for the eternal treasure will always reap a greater gain than any man made measurement.

> *"Give, and it shall be given unto you: good measure, pressed down, and shaken together, and running over, shall men give into your bosom. For with the same measure that ye mete withal it shall be measured to you again." Luke 6:38*

Givers give to get, to give, to get, to give, to get to....! What a magnificent principle. Our LORD, to whom we give, measures and metes righteously. One can not out give the LORD, so why not obey His leadership? Christianity and giving should be synonymous. A saved person will want to give and will be pleased in doing so because building treasures in the LORD is blessed of the LORD.

> *"..For unto whomsoever much is given, of him shall be much required..." Luke 12:48*

This is not an excuse to be relieved from giving from anyone who does not think he has much. The standard copout of "If I had more, then I would give more" does not measure up. I believe we are all accountable and if we are not obedient with little than we will not be obedient with much.

Although it is true that giving is a vital biblical principle, saving is also a biblical principle that is very important. One saving principle is to consider the ants when the time arrives to lie up in store.

> *"Go to the ant, thou sluggard; consider her ways, and be wise: Which having no guide, over-seer, or ruler, provideth her meat in the summer, and gathereth her food in the harvest." Proverbs 6:6-8*

The ants are self-motivated to understand the seasons. They are diligent to provide for their immediate needs and also to store up for the future.

Another profound saving principle is given to us in Genesis Forty One.

> *"And Joseph said unto Pharaoh, the dream of Pharaoh is one: God hath shewed Pharaoh what he is about to do. Now therefore let*

Kelle Hein

Pharaoh look out a man discreet and wise, and set him over the land of Egypt. Let Pharaoh do this, and let him appoint officers over the land and take up the fifth part of the land of Egypt in the seven plenteous years. And let them gather all the food of those good years that come, and lay up corn under the hand of Pharaoh, and let them keep food in the cities. And that food shall be for store to the land against the seven years of famine, which shall be in the land of Egypt; that the land perish not through the famine. And the thing was good in the eyes of Pharaoh, and in the eyes of all his servants. And Pharaoh said unto his servants, can we find such a one as this is, a man I whom the Spirit of God is? And Pharaoh said unto Joseph, forasmuch as God hath shewed thee all this; there is none so discreet and wise as thou art: Genesis 41:25, 33-39

Joseph reveals Pharaoh's amazing dream. In this context, we see the visible spiritual nature that Joseph possessed. An adherence to saving takes both discretion and wisdom. In the end, the twenty percent savings was the provision needed for Egypt's and Israel's sustainability. Would we be wise to apply the twenty percent saving principle?

Contrast another saving principle found in Exodus. We are made aware to beware and not get ahead of the LORD.

> *"Then said the LORD unto Moses, behold, I will rain bread from heaven for you; and the people shall go out and gather a certain rate every day, that I may prove them, whether they will walk in my law, or no. And it shall come to pass, that on the sixth day they shall prepare that which they bring in: and it shall be twice as much as they gather daily. This is the thing which the LORD hath commanded, gather of it every man according to his eating, an omer for every man, according to the number of your persons: take ye every man for them which are in his tents. And the children of Israel did so, and gathered some more, some less. And when they did mete it with an omer, he that gathered much had nothing over, and he that gathered little had no lack; they gathered every man according to his eating. And Moses said, let no man leave of it till the morning. Notwithstanding they hearkened not unto Moses: but some of them left of it until the morning, and it bred worms, and stank: and Moses was wroth with them. And they gathered it every morning, every man according to his eating: and when the sun waxed hot, it melted. And it came to*

pass, that on the sixth day they gathered twice as much bread, two omers for one man: and all the rulers of the congregation came and told Moses. And he said unto them, this is that which the LORD hath said, tomorrow is the rest of the holy Sabbath unto the LORD: bake that which ye will bake to day, and seethe that ye will seethe: and that which remaineth over lay up for you to be kept until the morning. And they laid it up till the morning, as Moses bade: and it did not stink, neither was there any worm therein. And Moses said, eat that to day; for to day ye shall not find it in the field. Six days ye shall gather it; but on the seventh day, which is the Sabbath, in it there shall be none. And it came to pass, that there went out some of the people on the seventh day for to gather, and they found none. And the LORD said unto Moses, how long refuse ye to keep my commandments and my laws?"
Exodus 16:4, 5, 16-28

Through the provision of manna, God showed the Israelites their dependence on the LORD and that he alone is their provider and blesser! The Israelites were told to gather what was sufficient for the day. Only on the sixth day were they to gather extra. Instead of trusting the LORD for his provision, they collected more than was needed. This act of human nature portrays a lack of obedience, trust, and faithlessness toward the one and only faithful GOD! Their distaste for integrity bred worms and rottenness. They wasted the allotted time to gather and failed to collect their provision in the appointed time!

Everyone should be saving a portion of their hard earned money. The "extra" account will always have a place to be spent. The occasional appliance failure, vehicle breakdown, and unexpected emergency are great reasons to have a "savings" fund. We all have our reasons why we save and how much we should save. No doubt money for retirement is a huge decision and is very relative to personal preference. Equally in people, churches should be wise in their expenditures. The attitude of local churches that continue to hoard money for a "rainy day," even though its facilities are well kept, sufficient and paid for, I believe is misplaced. The opportunities to spend wisely for mission projects are always prevalent and great. I do not believe the LORD is in the banking business just to collect but that His finances would be better allocated to advance the Kingdom of God! May we always remember who the real owner is!

The Building section of this financial chapter ends with a passage from the Book of Proverbs.

"The desire of the righteous is only good: but the expectation of the wicked is wrath. There is that scattereth, and yet increaseth; and there is that withholdeth more than is meet, but it tendeth to poverty. The liberal soul shall be made fat: and he that watereth shall

be watered also himself. He that withholdeth
corn, the people shall curse him: but blessing
shall be upon the head of him that selleth it."
Proverbs 11:23-26

Verse twenty-three states the final expectation of the wicked but, the righteous can enjoy continued good. Verse twenty four is a profound verse. To think that you can spread the blessings around and in return receive more blessings is huge. In contrast, to keep back or hold back is to have less. This is an awesome example of biblical addition and subtraction. We looked at Second Corinthians chapter nine and verse seven earlier but read verse six of the same chapter.

"But this I say, he which soweth sparingly
shall reap also sparingly; and he which
soweth bountifully shall reap also
bountifully."II Corinthians 9:6

As we search further through the Proverbs passage, we understand biblical mathematics better. Liberality is not a word that I normally aspire to but in this case; bring it on! It never ceases to amaze me how people justify themselves in the area of finances. They would love to have more but will not trust the LORD with what they have already. Also, they are content with just giving a little or just getting by and not experiencing the endless possibilities of what could be! Being a blessing is never a curse; it will only reciprocate more blessings.

BONDAGE

SAD STATE-

Many problematic circumstances have been created because of financial bondage. As the number one problem in marriage, finances have caused arguments and frustrations with couples. In addition, finances have caused family members to separate and friendships to end. The danger of borrowing and lending probably contributes to most of these problems.

The borrowing servant is enslaved to the lender until servitude is paid. What is a justifiable need to becoming a borrower? Each person should weigh out or count the cost before a decision of enslavement is made. Is it possible to keep a level head and still be under a burden? The supposed "need or desire" to "keep up with the Joneses" warps better judgment and thus allows lust to win over good sense. Too many "feelings" make financial decisions rather than sound financial judgment. Instead of money being a tool, it becomes a noose around one's neck. If everything was pay as you go then there would never be a problem but, we live in a credit using society.

"A good man sheweth favour and lendeth: he will guide his affairs with discretion." Psalms 112:5, "And if ye lend to them of whom ye hope to receive, what thank have ye? For sinners also lend to sinners, to receive as much again. But love ye your enemies, do good, and lend, hoping for nothing again; and your reward shall be great, and ye shall be the

children of the Highest: for he is kind unto the unthankful and to the evil." Luke 6:34, 35

Upon understanding these verses, I do not believe that the Bible teaches against lending and borrowing but, we must understand the heavy consequences that exist.

"The rich ruleth over the poor, and the borrower is servant to the lender." Proverbs 22:7

Servitude is created by those who have which are in contrast to those who have not. The person who is in need will know someone that can supply that need. The problem is that the borrower becomes subject to the lender. With this scenario, the bondage has begun.

SETTLING THE DEBT-

Romans 13:8 "Owe no man anything, but to love one another: for he that loveth another hath fulfilled the law."

Throughout the years, I have heard that this verse teaches that nobody should owe anybody anything. I'm not a proponent of debt because it definitely is bondage but, the context is about our love. Unadulterated love will fulfill all our obligations. A guilty verdict is our requirement to fulfill the sentence of love. True love will motivate and make this a reality in our life. May no one ever respond to us by saying "you did not love me". In contrast, the following verse dictates subjection to higher powers under GOD. These ministers of GOD were ordained to receive tribute. Although JESUS is the owner of the Temple, He paid a tribute to avoid offending them.

> *"And He said unto them, render therefore unto Caesar the things which be Caesar; and unto God the things which be God's"* Luke 20:25.

The Book of Matthew records money found in a fishes' mouth to pay a tribute. Do we owe a tax? We can argue the quantity but JESUS ordained the necessity. It is unfortunate that we whine about the government obligation but, we forget to glory in the godly opportunity to give to the LORD.

What other debts do we have? Has anyone ever owed an electric bill or water bill? We normally do not pay our utility bills in advance but, is it a debt? In these cases we are all indebted to someone. Certainly, the danger of borrowing can lead to bondage but any payment to a lender under a predetermined time and amount is still considered a debt. In this context, even rent or a lease should be considered debt.

When money is available for monthly payments, is it still considered to be outside the bondage realm? Is it "real" debt only when you cannot pay the monthly payment? Can you be under the "bondage" control even if you can pay on time? We normally do not think of ourselves being under financial bondage when we can pay our bills but, the pressure of the payment can be bondage.

Anytime lending is involved or the full price of a product is unpaid then a debt is owed. Anyone that accomplishes a service without getting paid immediately causes a debt. The bondage begins until we can settle the debt.

Is interest (usury) a problem or a good play?

"Wherefore then gavest not thou my money into the bank, that at my coming I might have required mine own with usury?" Luke 19:23.

This verse encourages increasing your investment with interest. I call it a good play when receiving interest but, a problem when paying interest.

"Thou shalt not lend upon usury to thy brother: usury of money, usury of victuals, usury of anything that is lent upon usury: Unto a stranger thou mayest lend upon usury; but unto thy brother thou shalt not lend upon usury: that the LORD thy GOD may bless thee in all that thou settest thine hand to in the land whither thou goest to possess it." Deuteronomy 23:19, 20

We are told that a stranger could be charged usury but not unto a brother. This Old Testament principle teaches us to not charge your brother interest for borrowed money. My personal practice is to not lend money at all. When I'm asked and if I'm able, I just give the money. I say "This is a gift, as unto the LORD, and nothing is owed back". This will alleviate any attitude of keeping anyone under bondage. In Nehemiah chapter five, we read about a serious case of bondage exacted.

> *"Some also there were that said, we have mortgaged our lands, vineyards, and houses, that we might buy corn, because of the dearth. There were also that said, we have borrowed money for the king's tribute, and that upon our lands and vineyards. Yet now our flesh is as the flesh of our brethren, our children as their children: and, lo, we bring into bondage our sons and our daughters to be servants, and are brought unto bondage already: neither is it in our power to redeem them; for other men have our hands and vineyards. And I was very angry when I heard their cry and these words. Then I consulted with myself, and I rebuked the nobles, and rulers, and said unto them, ye exact usury, every one of his brother. And I set a great assembly against them. And I said unto them. We after our ability have redeemed our brethren the Jews, which were sold unto the heathen; and will ye even sell your brethren? Or shall they be sold unto us? Then held they their peace, and found nothing to answer. Also I said, it is*

not good that ye do: ought ye not to walk in the fear of our God because of the reproach of the heathen our enemies? I likewise, and my brethren, and my servants, might exact of them money and corn: I pray you, let us leave off this usury. Restore, I pray you, to them, even this day, their lands, their vineyards, their oliveyards, and their houses, also the hundredth part of the money, and of the corn, the wine, and the oil, that ye exact of them."
Nehemiah 5:3-11

A dearth created the mortgaging of all possessions and usury was charged. The people were under great duress and unity was thwarted. Nehemiah reminded them against charging usury and bringing their brethren under bondage. Clearer heads prevailed and in the end, total restoration was enacted.

The personal question that still remains is what does bondage mean to you? Each individual will classify or justify their personal situation. Debt in any form or fashion will have consequences and be burdensome on many different levels. There are multiple benefits to giving but, if someone is in debt, their ability to give will be greatly hindered. The best way to always have your debts paid is to not have a debt!

SETTLING THE SCORE-

We live in a "sue" happy society. When the courtroom gets involved, a small problem can become a big deal. Lost (unjust) people will do what lost people do but, the scriptural principle for saved brethren is to settle a matter and to remain outside the courtroom. Financial gains or losses should not involve the brethren in a court of law against one another.

> *"Dare any of you, having a matter against another, go to law before the unjust, and not before the saints? Do ye not know that the saints shall judge the world? And if the world shall be judged by you, are ye unworthy to judge the smallest matters? Know ye not that we shall judge angels? How much more things that pertain to this life? If then ye have judgments of things pertaining to this life, set them to judge who are least esteemed in the church. I speak to your shame. Is it so, that there is not a wise man among you? no, not one that shall be able to judge between his brethren? But brother goeth to law with brother, and that before the unbelievers. Now therefore there is utterly a fault among you, because ye go to law one with another, Why do ye not rather take wrong? Why do ye not rather suffer yourselves to be defrauded?*

Kelle Hein

Nay, ye do wrong, and defraud, and that your brethren." 1 Corinthians 6:1-8

After reading this scripture passage, is there any justification for a believer to take another brother to court? As saints, what matters most is to keep everything in perspective. While looking ahead to judge the world and fallen angels, why can't we settle a small matter? To the wise, certainly, the negative outcome of taking the brethren to court screams the obvious. What makes matters worse is the testimony of embarrassment. An unjust person will be exposed to divisiveness within the brethren. True love amongst the brethren will be affected and will hinder the reception of CHRIST's love to the unjust. In the end, who matters most? It is better to act humble and suffer wrongfully. The cause of CHRIST is at stake and the cost "just to be right" is too great!

SURETY-

Many horror stories have been lived out for being a surety. Anytime we become a financial stability for someone else, we have the potential for financial suffering. Whether it is friend or foe, stranger or acquaintance, we are ill advised to bring ourselves under someone else's debt.

"My son if thou be surety for thy friend, if thou hast stricken thy hand with a stranger, thou art snared with the words of thy mouth, thou art taken with the words of thy mouth. Do this now, my son, and deliver thyself,

when thou art come into the hand of thy friend; go, humble thyself, and make sure thy friend. Give not sleep to thine eyes, nor slumber to thine eyelids. Deliver thyself as roe from the hand of the hunter, and as a bird from the hand of the fowler." Proverbs 6:1-5

Do you remember the days when your hand shake would seal a deal? Such is the bond of financial security when we fall prey to a smooth talking friend about a good idea. Because of our relationship, and our own agreeing words, we entrap ourselves to help carry the financial load. When you endure that ill feeling in your gut, you know that the snare has been made. We think that denying a friend will hinder a friendship but true friendship should not be bound with finances. Regardless of the cost, we should not lose sleep over the situation but gracefully and humbly decline the suretiship. Real rest will not be attained until there is an escape from the financial death trap. Without question, many financial partnerships have gone well, but the negative potential is not worth losing a friendship. The best scenario is to avoid the emotional spanking of being a surety.

SCHEMING-

Financial extortion has long been a human and historical trait. Governments, politicians, and individuals have all been guilty of playing the extortion game. The Bible gives an example in Luke chapter nineteen.

Kelle Hein

"And when they saw it, they all murmured, saying, that he was gone to be guest with a man that is a sinner. And Zacchaeus stood, and said unto the LORD; behold, LORD, the half of my goods I give to the poor: and if I have taken anything from any man by false accusation, I restore him fourfold. And Jesus said unto him, this day is salvation come to this house, forsomuch as he also is a son of Abraham. For the Son of man is come to seek and to save that which was lost."
Luke 19:7-10

A publican man named Zacchaeus had an occupation that allowed him to abuse his position. The taxes that he collected were more than the allotted government's "fair" share. Zacchaeus abused his authority to climb the economic social ladder but in doing so, his general social acceptance was lowered. After receiving the greatest gift that money could not buy, he wanted to correct the misuse of his occupation. He began to bless others by giving instead of taking. Zacchaeus expressed his generous desire to the poor by restoring 400 percent of anything that he had falsely received. He followed an Old Testament principle (Leviticus. 6:1-7) and became an example to prove that his heart had been changed. This tax collector had schemed money through false accusations and unlawful means but his changed heart manifested in a fourfold restoration.

Scheming, false gain, greed, authoritative power, etc. will never be satisfied after a godly conscience is received.

> *"Thou shalt not defraud thy neighbour, neither rob him: the wages of him that is hired shall not abide with thee all night until the morning." Leviticus 19:13*

Anyone that has ever worked a job and then was not paid at the proper time can relate to being manipulated. When an employer holds out payment for no particular reason, the employee feels used. This Old Testament verse from Leviticus dictates a principle for timely payment. Making prior arrangements is one thing but, even waiting to the next day is considered a rip off. In the past, I have been strung out for too long to receive payment on a finished job. Nonpayment does not get better with delay or procrastination.

> *"Go to now, ye rich men, weep and howl for your miseries that shall come upon you. Your riches are corrupted, and your garments are moth eaten. Your gold and silver is cankered; and the rust of them shall be a witness against you, and shall eat your flesh as it were fire. Ye have heaped treasure together for the last days. Behold the fire of the labourers who have reaped down your fields, which are of you kept back by fraud, crieth: and the cries of them which have reaped are entered into the ears of the Lord of Sabaoth." James 5:1-4*

This New Testament passage relates a classic example of riches obtained by fraud. Riches can bring a man to his ruin. In the process of attaining wealth, a person can lose sight of what is important. Without the laborers, the outcome could not be attained. Instead of reaping a great treasure, fraudulent practices reaped the ire of the hire. The proprietors' selfishness spoke even unto the Lord of Sabaoth (military might). Money acquired from unpaid laborers will not reap a lasting benefit.

We all want to be accepted. In CHRIST, we are already accepted in the beloved but; the desire to keep up with the "Joneses" still hangs around.

> *"But a certain man named Ananias, with Sapphira his wife, sold a possession, and kept back part of the price, his wife also being privy to it, and brought a certain part, and laid it at the apostles' feet. But Peter said, Ananias, why hath Satan filled thine heart to lie to the Holy Ghost, and to keep back part of the price of the land? Whiles it remained, was it not thine own? And after it was sold, was it not in thine own power? Why hast thou conceived this thing in thine heart? Thou hast not lied unto men, but unto God. And Ananias hearing these words fell down, and gave up the ghost: and great fear came on all them that heard these things" Acts 5:1-5*

These scriptures reveal a striking truth about the lack of financial integrity. In the preceding chapter, people were selling possessions and using the proceeds to help others. Ananias and his wife Sapphira wanted to join in on the blessings and be known for their philanthropy. While they were under no obligation to quantify the sale, they proclaimed to have given all the proceeds for distribution. The truth was that only a portion was given. Peter knew the truth and caught them in a greedy lie. Deception became their downfall and death was their end.

I will end scheming with bribery.

> *"And thou shalt take no gift: for the gift blindeth the wise, and perverteth the word of the righteous" Exodus 23:8; "And said to the judges, Take heed what ye do: for ye judge not for man, but for the LORD, who is with you in the judgment. Wherefore now let the fear of the LORD be upon you; take heed and do it: for there is no iniquity with the LORD our GOD, nor respect of person, nor taking of gifts,"   II Chronicles 19:6, 7*

This financial cancer still exists and is a biblical human reality. Money has long been used to blind an eye. Bribery is a form of bondage because manipulation can be used to change an opinion about evidence against someone else. Many a ploy has been attempted to change a personal or political outcome. If one can buy off or be paid off, then they become a respecter of persons and true judgment will be thwarted!

> *"Now when they were going, behold, some of the watch came into the city, and shewed unto the chief priests all the things that were done. And when they were assembled with the elders, and had taken counsel, they gave large money unto the soldiers, saying, say ye, His disciples came by night, and stole him away while we slept. And if this come to the governor's ears, we will persuade him, and secure you. So they took the money, and did as they were taught; and this saying is commonly reported among the Jews until this day." Matthew 28:11-15*

It is amazing that even to the very end of Christ Jesus' earthly ministry bribery was perpetrated. Instead of telling the truth, lies were invented. In this instance, greed meshed with bribery and this same falsification continues today. The lies and deception have a tendency to grow bigger and be carried farther. Money can be a tremendous tool for righteousness but, when man is involved; the tool can become used and abused for unrighteousness.

BLESSINGS-

As I write this section, I remember many of the personal blessings with a financial connotation. When a legitimate matter was due, we have received many overwhelming offerings that were sent by the LORD right on time. Our family has experienced blessings that were not visible in a bank account but could be distinctly quantified. We have been given tools, vehicles and airplanes. We prayed to build a debt free home and our LORD honored that prayer. Although we have never had a large bank account, honestly, we have been financially and tremendously blessed. I have never wanted to measure my ability or availability by our bank account size. Living by faith and doing the ministry without the visible necessary funds has been awesome! Whatever our LORD has led us in, He has provided! Finances are from the LORD and He has a bountiful supply. To be sure, our LORD has blessed us more than we deserve!

Regardless of the opportunity, no withdrawal is too big from GOD's bank account.

> *"But my God shall supply all your need according to his riches in glory by Christ Jesus." Phil 4:19.*

This is a tremendous promise given to the local church at Philippi. There will never be an end to the unlimited resources that are in CHRIST JESUS. Not only does our LORD own the cattle on a thousand hills (Ps 50:12); He owns the hills also!

The LORD has demonstrated His abundance many times and He is able to produce any return on an investment.

> *"Then Isaac sowed in that land, and received in the same year an hundredfold: and the*

LORD blessed him. And the man waxed great, and went forward, and grew until he became very great: For he had possession of flocks, and possession of herds, and great store of servants: and the Philistines envied him." Genesis 26:12-14

Isaac, in one years' time, received a ten thousand percent increase and was tremendously blessed. He became known for his great influence, purpose and obedience for the LORD! Without question, another book would need to be written for the life of Solomon who is still the wealthiest man to ever live (II Chronicles 1:12).

Do we really appreciate our blessings? It would behoove us to never let the blessings go to our head. Is it not all about perspective? May we have a keen eye and a clear head when it comes to our blessings. All of our blessings are undeserved and nothing we do merits anything.

"But by the grace of God, I am what I am"
I Corinthians 15:10a.

The following passage will contrast the potential best case scenario and the obvious worst case scenario.

"I went by the field of the slothful, and by the vineyard of the man void of understanding; and, lo, it was all grown over with thorns, and nettles had covered the face thereof, and the stone wall thereof was broken down Then I saw, and considered it well: I looked upon it,

and received instruction. Yet a little sleep, a little slumber, a little folding of the hands to sleep: So shall thy poverty come as one that travelleth; and thy want as an armed man."
Proverbs 24:30-34

We read about a field, vineyard and a stone wall. This man, as a steward, is responsible to utilize the possessions given to him as blessings. You and I may not have these particular possessions but too often we undervalue the ones we do have. In reality, they belong to the LORD and they are not toys or "feel good" trinkets. Our blessings should be respected because what we have received is what we are responsible for. Unfortunately, we "belittle the blessings". Many times our attitude and outlook does not portray appreciation. Without diligence and steadfastness, the man in Proverbs twenty four was exposed to the enemy. Slothfulness allowed the wall to be broken and his protection was breached. The planted fruit and grain should have been visible but, they were not. Slothfulness allowed the thorns and nettles to be seen as ungratefulness. Bearing fruit is a blessing but in contrast yielding thorns and nettles are a curse. When we do not count the costs, we will let undone tasks become tomorrow's burdens. Obviously this man was unwilling to understand his instruction. Instead of abundance, little by little his laziness produced waste. Without any concern for the opportunistic potential, his slothfulness left him impoverished and powerless!

All in all, finances are from the LORD! The only reason that we have anything is because He gave! In the end, it is really very simple.

> *"And Jacob vowed a vow, saying. If God will be with me, and will keep me in this way that I go, and will give me bread to eat, and raiment to put on, so that I come again to my father's house in peace; then shall the LORD be my GOD" Genesis 28:20, 21*

Can it be anymore simple than food and raiment? As He is your LORD, then everything else outside of food and raiment is a bona fide blessing!

> *"But seek ye first the kingdom of God, and his righteousness; and all these things shall be added unto you." Matthew 6:33*

What's The Bible Got To Do With It?

FISHING

Fishermen follow a hunch or a gut feeling. It may be that favorite spot or "old faithful" place that has always produced fish. Fishing, with all its variables, is very complex. Many things come together in the right way at the right time. It's always a challenge to "out smart" the fish. With the right tackle, technique, and timing, fish can be caught. Unfortunately, many times we have all experienced the dilemma that the fish get fed and not us.

We all know that tools are important and having the right tools for the right job brings about the most efficiency. In fishing, you can have the best boat, trolling motor, depth finder, net, poles, etc. If you cannot use them correctly, you will not be as successful. In fishing for men, we have the greatest tool that exists. In fact, it is out of this world in effectiveness. From a biblical stand point, when the fish (men) accept the bait, then the Bible is the only tool that matters. The Bible is the tool that tells man that he has hunger and also satisfies that hunger. This tool is the only one that will work to become a successful "fisher of men". In order to become a follower and fisher of men, it behooves us to know and understand the Bible better.

What's The Bible Got To Do With It?

"And Jesus, walking by the sea of Galilee, saw two brethren, Simon called Peter, and Andrew his brother, casting a net into the sea: for they were fishers. And he saith unto them, Follow me, and I will make you fishers of men. And they straightway left their nets, and followed him." Matthew 4:18-20

These verses reveal a call for fishing and an immediate response to that call. Simon and Andrew did not hesitate; and neither should we!

Fishing is a great relaxing sport but it has some even greater spiritual applications. In reality, no one would be saved without somebody fishing. The scripture uses the term "fishers of men" and it is not just a play on words but, a very serious endeavor. Being a fisherman can be an occupation or a pastime but, a "fisher of men" should be a lifestyle. The avid fisherman does what it takes to catch fish and this same attitude should be manifested in fishing for men! The LORD JESUS CHRIST called fishermen to be "fishers of men" and they followed him.

Tackle is a vital part of fishing and I remember having several different hooks, lures, spinners, artificial worms, etc in my tackle box. All of these things would travel with me to every fishing hole. The spiritual tackle box is the Holy Spirit.

"Wherefore I give you to understand, that no man speaking by the Spirit of God calleth Jesus accursed: and that no man can say that

Kelle Hein

Jesus is the Lord, but by the Holy Ghost." I Corinthians 12:3

Without the tackle box, fishing is futile. Likewise, without the Holy Spirit, effective fishing for men is vain. Each unique tackle is used for a specific purpose and for an appropriate time. Whenever I went fishing, if any one of the tackle was not in the box, it seemed that that was the one that I needed. If a dedicated fisherman would have everything at his disposal to be the most effective, then so much the more, would a fisher of men need to be prepared. Respectfully, the Holy Spirit knows our assets and effectiveness in order to catch men. The reason that you went fishing is to catch fish, right?

We have all been around an individual or another boat that has similar bait and tackle and while you are right next to them… well, you know the end of this story! Why do they catch the fish? Did I bob it right or let it bounce correctly? Did I set the hook, pull then set, wait more, ugh! Obviously, the right technique is crucial to catching fish. Different fish are caught in different ways. The level of experience will help to dictate which technique to use. Interestingly, men come in all shapes and sizes and they all get caught using diverse strategies. The Holy Spirit will always utilize the best technique. The apostle Paul writes about some great tactics for fishing men.

"To the weak became I as weak that I might gain the weak: I am made all things to all men, that I might by all means save some"
I Corinthians 9:22

This biblical fishing principal teaches us that people are on distinct levels and come from various back grounds. They are open or closed, aware or distracted, enlightened or annoyed and on and on it goes with fishing humanity. Technique will depend on the mood and situation within the fishing hole of men.

"And this I do for the gospel's sake, that I might be partaker thereof with you."
I Corinthians 9:23

By integrating every available technique possible, each fishing opportunity will receive the best possible effort to catch men. Every person that is fished should receive the best cast in order to be caught. Even the LORD JESUS CHRIST used a different approach to accomplish a positive result. The woman at the well in John chapter four, the farmer sowing the seed in Matthew chapter thirteen, the rich young ruler in Luke chapter eighteen, and the fishermen catching fish in Matthew chapter four, etc.; these were all dealt distinctly one from another.

Many variances of times and seasons exist in fishing. It takes discernment and wisdom to know when the fish will bite. In life, men are bound by times and seasons also. As with men, even the best fishing time does not mean the fish will take the bait. Both fishing bait and biblical bait can be rejected. In learning to fish one must understand habits, preferences, feeding patterns, whether it is calm water, a raging river, on the bottom or near the top. Fishing for men is equally important. People have likes and dislikes and respond in many ways. Knowing that people are fickle and moody, our insight is crucial to enhance fishing skills.

When we go fishing are we ready to catch fish? Why is the big fish that got away always the biggest story? Preparation, readiness, and discernment are paramount to ensure that no fish get away. How vital is it to set the hook or draw the net? An unset hook can be spit out and a mishandled net can repel and lose fish. If we do not take time to mend and maintain the net, then our stringer will remain empty. Should anything less be expected when fishing for men? The most effective "fisher of men" will have his/her attitude and willingness mended and maintained.

> *"Now when he had left speaking, he said unto Simon, Launch out into the deep, and let down your nets for a draught. And Simon answering said unto him, Master, we have toiled all the night, and have taken nothing: nevertheless at thy word I will let down the net. And when they had this done, they enclosed a great multitude of fishes: and their net brake." Luke 5:4-6*

What's The Bible Got To Do With It?

Simon had fished all night and while he was cleaning his nets Jesus commanded him to go out again. Although the depth and the daylight were contrary to his expertise and expectation, he still obeyed. Yet being tired, Simon thrust out to trust Jesus' word and received a great treasure of fish. Instead of letting down nets, their disobedience incurred a repair cost. How many more fish would have total obedience harvested?

When will you draw the net? Do we have the right tackle using the right technique and availability for the right time? Are we ready to go fishing? When someone asks me to go fishing, I like to hear "I have already hooked up the boat to the truck". This attitude shows expedience and readiness.

> *"...Fear not; from henceforth thou shalt catch men." Luke 5:10*

Jesus was alluding to the future need for all men to be caught. Physical fishing is from life to death but, spiritual fishing is from death to life, amen! I like to fish but, am I a "fisher of men"? The Bible allows me to see that an everyday "hobby" can have eternal results through the "fishing" principle. I am so thankful that someone went fishing for me!

FORGIVENESS

I find it very interesting that forgiveness is a word that can be both received and granted. Anyone can possess and administer forgiveness. Webster's Dictionary states that to "forgive" is to pardon; remit as a sin, offense, debt, etc.: to exhibit forgiveness.[1] Unfortunately, for too many people, to give a pardon and remit a sin, offense and debt is easier said than done! Is not the whole point of forgiveness for giving? No doubt everyone desires to receive the wonderful gift of forgiveness but many times it is not as readily given. When we have been wronged, the right thing to do is to be asked for our forgiveness, right? On the other hand, when we wrong another person, are we as quick to ask forgiveness? Our desire to receive a pardon may not be met with the same fervor to give a pardon. The action to either give or receive forgiveness becomes a choice. With that choice, do we give slack depending on the person at fault or hold a grudge beyond forgiveness? Much care needs to be taken in order to uphold consistent forgiveness.

Is everything forgivable? One might say "Well that depends on what it is". We try and justify forgiveness through the spectrum of "is it deserved". Remember, if it is only about deserving forgiveness, nobody would ever be forgiven. The requested forgiveness will never measure up to merit! That is why forgiveness is for giving.

Have you ever heard "go ahead and do it because it is easier to ask forgiveness than to ask permission"? Although that may be true, it does not make the action justifiable. The statement "forgive me" should be genuine; conversely, too often the person asking to be forgiven knowingly will have to ask again. Should you blindly and mentally forgive the person when he hides a wrong motive? Committing a wrong still has consequences. Biblically, concerning forgiveness, we are given many examples about consequential choices. Of course you forgive but, does that mean that you should compromise and violate scriptural principles? Forgiveness is serious and it is not a game. When we give or receive forgiveness it must be real!

Giving and receiving forgiveness is very emotional. Both physical and spiritual forgiveness are verifiable. I have received and I have given human forgiveness. Spiritually, I have received a pardon and through the Spirit of God I have granted forgiveness. True forgiveness is from the LORD. Honestly, only the LORD can give you the grace and ability to look above and beyond the idiocy of man! The most absurd and egregious faults of man have been forgiven, amen! I am especially thankful that my folly has been forgiven.

The one thing that is not forgivable is unbelief. The Bible is very clear that unforgiveness is received through unbelief.

Kelle Hein

"He that believeth on him is not condemned: but he that believeth not is condemned already, because he hath not believed in the name of the only begotten Son of God." John 3:18, "Wherefore I say unto you, All manner of sin and blasphemy shall be forgiven unto men: but the blasphemy against the Holy Ghost shall not be forgiven unto men. And whosoever speaketh a word against the Son of man, it shall be forgiven him: but whosoever speaketh against the Holy Ghost, it shall not be forgiven him, neither in this world, neither in the world to come." Matthew 12:31, 32

Condemnation is the opposite of commendation and unbelief is never commendable. Christ Jesus is the giver of eternal life. The Holy Spirit brings the gift of life to fallen man. Blaspheming the Son is forgiven but blaspheming the Spirit is unforgivable. Unbelief denies the essence of God and the opportunity for salvation.

REJOICE-

Again, this is why forgiveness is for giving. The LORD JESUS CHRIST himself has already unequivocally forgiven everyone that has lived or will ever have life! In Him, we have forgiveness! Do you believe it?

"In whom we have redemption through his blood, the forgiveness of sins, according to the riches of his grace:" Ephesians 1:7, "In

157

whom we have redemption through his blood,
even the forgiveness of sins:" Colossians 1:14

Redemption and forgiveness is praise worthy. This truth should be shouted from the house tops. Rejoicing in forgiveness is not a hope so, think so, or maybe possession. Too many are still trying to acquire their forgiveness. We are guilty of sin but JESUS has taken the penalty of sin away. When people deny the gift of forgiveness, they are trying to clean up their own fallen state. My question is "What will you do with your sin?" The end of sin is still death.

"But every man is tempted, when he is drawn
away of his own lust, and enticed. Then when
lust hath conceived, it bringeth forth sin: and
sin, when it is finished, bringeth forth death."
James 1:14, 15

Our sin guilt can not be cleared by ourselves. JESUS died, was buried, and rose from the dead to give eternal life. Otherwise, we would just be a forgiven dead person because without the resurrection there would be no life!

"For he hath made him to be sin for us, who
knew no sin: that we might be made the
righteousness of God in him." II Corinthians
5:21, "That if thou shalt confess with thy
mouth the LORD JESUS, and shalt believe in
thine heart that GOD hath raised him from
the dead, thou shalt be saved." Romans 10:9,

"For GOD so loved the world, that he gave his only begotten Son, that whosoever believeth in him should not perish, but have everlasting life." John 3:16

As a pilot, I remember entering through the airport security gate many times. Upon waiving my security badge and then entering my code, the gate would open. Immediately, I would read on the screen the word "accepted". This would trigger a wonderful memory of my position in the LORD.

"To the praise of the glory of his grace, wherein he hath make us accepted in the beloved." Ephesians 1:6

He has accepted me because he has forgiven me. Can you hear me shouting right now? Hallelujah to the LORD for giving forgiveness! Our ability to rejoice is not based on us or anything we will ever do. Our forgiveness is a gift from the LORD. Any other motive for rejoicing is vanity and self-reliant.

The greatest forgiveness example given is when the LORD JESUS CHRIST hung on the cross.

"Then said JESUS, Father, forgive them; for they know not what they do. And they parted his raiment, and cast lots." Luke 23:34

Even in the very moment of giving forgiveness, He asked for them to be forgiven!

What's The Bible Got To Do With It?

"Rejoice in the LORD always: and again I say, Rejoice." Philippians 4:4

Can you see any reason not to rejoice?

RECKON-

The act of reckoning is to take inventory or make a computation. In aviation, we use a term called "dead reckoning." Calculations are made and visible references are used to verify whether you are in the right position. The critical question is "Are you on the correct course?"

"Likewise reckon ye also yourselves to be dead indeed unto sin, but alive unto God through Jesus Christ our Lord. Let not sin therefore reign in your mortal body, that ye should obey it in the lusts thereof."
Romans 6:11, 12

We are reckoned dead in sin, but because of salvation, we are alive in JESUS CHRIST! Each person must understand that there is a day of reckoning.

"The wicked flee when no man pursueth: but the righteous are bold as a lion."
Proverbs 28:1

The guilty person has a tendency to "look over his shoulder" lest he get caught. Usually, when people are guilty they avoid anyone or anything connected with the wrong. Guilt has a way of controlling one's life however; it can be used for a positive result. One does not have to remain guilty. One can accept his position and choose a new course. The new direction changes your whole perspective.

When guilt no longer dominates our actions, we can walk with boldness and freedom! As humans, the enemy is our humanity. We try to accomplish something for the eternal with the temporal or something spiritual with the physical. True reckoning will live for the LORD and not lust for self.

> *"But if we walk in the light, as he is in the light, we have fellowship one with another, and the blood of Jesus Christ his Son cleanseth us from all sin. If we say that we have no sin, we deceive ourselves, and the truth is not in us. If we confess our sins, he is faithful and just to forgive us our sins, and to cleanse us from all unrighteousness. If we say that we have not sinned, we make him a liar, and his word is not in us."*
> *I John 1:7-10*

I reckon myself alive unto God but, living in this sinful body is a constant battle. Because we are sinners, we are never outside the state of sinfulness. The blood of JESUS CHRIST not only saves eternally from the penalty of sin but, it also cleanses us moment by moment. To act like we do not need cleansing is ignorant and to say that the LORD needs not to cleanse us is ignominy. We acknowledge our sin by confessing in response to the LORD's cleansing. Since we certainly have no right to challenge the forgiving ability of the LORD, why would we tempt the LORD to prove his forgiveness?

> *"And it came to pass, after the year was expired, at the time when kings go forth to battle, that David sent Joab, and his servants with him, and all Israel; and they destroyed the children of Ammon, and besieged Rabbah. But David tarried still at Jerusalem. And it came to pass in an eveningtide that David arose from off his bed, and walked upon the roof of the king's house: and from the roof he saw a woman washing herself; and the woman was very beautiful to look upon. And David sent and enquired after the woman. And one said, Is not this Bath-sheba, the daughter of Eliam, the wife of Uriah the Hittite? And David sent messengers, and took her; and she came in unto him, and he lay with her; for she was purified from her uncleanness: and she returned unto her house. And the woman conceived, and sent and told David, and said I am with child...And it came to pass in the morning, that David wrote a letter to Joab, and sent it by the hand of Uriah. And he wrote in the letter, saying, Set ye Uriah in the forefront of the hottest battle, and retire ye from him, that he may be smitten, and die...And when the*

*wife of Uriah heard that Uriah her husband
was dead, she mourned for her husband. And
when the mourning was past, David sent and
fetched her to his house, and she became his
wife, and bare him a son. But the thing that
David had done displeased the LORD."
II Samuel 12:1-5, 14, 15, 26, 27*

King David is probably one of the most recognized
person in the Bible. Although King David was a man after
God's own heart, he had his own moments to be reckoned.
King David's lack of discipline pales in comparison to most.
David gave over to the lust of the flesh and he became a
slave to his decision. The results were adultery, a conceived
child and premeditated murder. The cover up was futile and
the LORD was not pleased!

*"Know ye not, that to whom ye yield
yourselves servants to obey, his servants ye
are to whom ye obey; whether of sin unto
death, or of obedience unto righteousness?"
Romans 6:16*

In a moment of weakness, David gave in to unholy
feelings and sustained the consequences. To yield unto
obedient righteousness is one thing, but unto unrighteousness
is another thing all together. Of course, the LORD knows
everything, but soon enough, everyone else knew. David's
sin was no longer a secret and he suffered greatly.

"For thou didst it secretly: but I will do this thing before all Israel, and before the sun."
II Samuel 12:12

Although many other consequences followed, David finally took responsibility and endured the chastisement.

"And David said unto Nathan, I have sinned against the LORD. And Nathan said unto David, The LORD also hath put away thy sin; thou shalt not die. Howbeit, because by this deed thou hast given great occasion to the enemies of the LORD to blaspheme, the child also that is born unto thee shall surely die. And he said, While the child was yet alive. I fasted and wept: for I said, Who can tell whether God will be gracious to me, that the child may live? And David comforted Bathsheba his wife, and went in unto her, and lay with her: and she bare a son, and he called his name Solomon: and the LORD loved him." II Samuel 12:13, 14, 22, 24

This is where a real case of reckoning took place. The child died and David's reputation was tarnished but he continued to let reproof yield fasting, prayer and worship. He relied totally on the LORD and through the grace of GOD he was rewarded with the birth of Solomon. We can vividly see how one lustful action that produced egregious sin can set up forgiveness and restoration precedence. In the beginning, David delayed the great opportunity to be forgiven but, once he admitted his wrong and repented, forgiveness was received. Guilt is the obvious emotion that should drive us to receive forgiveness. I reckon it is so much more wonderful to live in forgiveness than guilt. Being forgiven is worthy for both rejoicing and reckoning.

RECEIVE and RECIPROCATE-

Human interaction constantly creates different reactions. How often have you wondered if someone was mad or upset from their facial expression? Instead, they were just deep in thought. We may perceive wrongly an indifferent look or a tone in a voice and get a bad attitude. Someone may spout out a remark and think it is cute when really it is a cut. We think it is ok to cover up cutting words with a chuckle or laugh but, it is still an offense. The old cliché "sticks and stones can break my bones but, words will never hurt me" is a lie! "News flash", we do not always have to say what we are thinking! If we do not think before we speak or react to a situation, then spoken words or a sneering look will be very hurtful and quite damaging.

People that have been wronged have a hard time moving forward and by contrast a guilty person has just as much difficulty forgiving himself. The common response is "let it go" or "get over it," but this is easier said than done. The challenge to forgive will manifest itself mightily through these human interactions. The challenge to pass the "will you forgive me" and "I forgive you" test will be confronted. When one truly understands the power of forgiveness, they can have fun with how easy it is to forgive. Granting forgiveness is very liberating and the expression on people's faces is priceless. Anyway, forgiveness is always more enjoyable than living with bitterness, spite, a grudge or unforgiveness, amen.

> *"Woe unto the world because of offences! For it must needs be that offences come; but woe to that man by whom the offence cometh! Moreover if thy brother shall trespass against thee, go and tell him his fault between thee and him alone: if he shall hear thee, thou hast gained thy brother. But if he will not hear thee, then take with thee one or two more, that in the mouth of two or three witnesses every work may be established. And if he shall neglect to hear them, tell it unto the church: but if he neglect to hear the church, let him be unto thee as an heathen man and a publican. Verily I say unto you, Whatsoever ye shall bind on earth shall be bound in heaven: and whatsoever ye shall loose on earth shall be loosed in heaven. Again I say unto you, That if two of you shall agree on earth as touching anything that they shall ask, it shall be done for them of my Father which is in heaven."*
> *Matthew 18:7, 15-19*

What a powerful scripture that shows how trespasses and offences create havoc with feelings. Either, consciously or unconsciously, offences are real and they must be dealt with. This vivid example is played out many times in humanity. Regardless of the fault, the offense has been committed and a close relationship has been breached.

> *A brother offended is harder to be won than a*
> *strong city; and their contentions are like the*
> *bars of a castle." Proverbs 18:19*

Knowing this makes it more difficult to deal with and talk to an offended brother. He has his fortified walls up and is hard to reach.

In order to amend a problem, three things must come to fruition. The first one is action. It is ironic that the trespassed (offended) brother is to make the first move. The offender is not a mind reader and usually has no idea that an offense has been committed. The offended brother has a choice to be offended and then takes responsible action to give the offender the opportunity to apologize.

Secondly, there is an attitude with the action. The whole point about an offense is to gain your brother back. The offended brother informs the offender and tells him his fault.

> *"Brethren, if a man be overtaken in a fault, ye*
> *which are spiritual, restore such a one in the*
> *spirit of meekness; considering thyself, lest*
> *thou also be tempted." Galatians 6:1*

How do we handle someone that has fallen in sin? A profound truth is given to have an attitude of humility. Even a "spiritual" brother can fall in temptation. *"Restore"* comes from a medical term meaning to "set a broken bone". Certainly, a caretaking attitude is paramount for gaining a brother.

When the offended brother makes the offense known, the offender should gladly apologize and be thankful to restore the relationship. I do not read that the offended brother should leave, throw a fit, be absent, get a bad attitude, etc; but, to make the first move and then each person resolves the relationship breach. If this is not possible, do not get offended!

Thirdly, accountability is crucial. If the first move is unsuccessful than take two or three others to be witnesses. If unsuccessful again, then the matter needs to be taken before the church. Now, what was done in secret is totally out in the open. The church is bound under authority to put everything in order. The churches unity is at stake and the seriousness of togetherness must be maintained.

The unrepentant brother (offender) is to receive discipline. *"Neglect to hear"* is the point. If the offender leaves, then hearing is neglected. Even though the right action is taken with the right attitude, accountability reveals whether the offender will act spiritual. Hearing will heed harmony. Misplaced hearing will not breed hatred but, restoration will still be missing. Is it not easier just to ask for and receive forgiveness?

The word forgiveness is never mentioned in Matthew chapter 18; however, it screams for the act of forgiveness. Of course, forgiveness is never withheld, right? Once again, the two-sided reality to receive and reciprocate forgiveness comes to light.

> *"And be ye kind one to another, tenderhearted, forgiving one another, even as God for Christ's sake hath forgiven you."* *Ephesians 4:32*

Our forgiveness is unconditionally given to us from the LORD JESUS CHRIST. The necessity to forgive and be forgiven is accomplished in this one verse. Without a doubt, we can be assured that our forgiveness is secure. Therefore, we are accountable to apply the same truth and grant forgiveness to an offender.

> *"Then came Peter to him, and said, Lord, how oft shall my brother sin against me, and I forgive him? Till seven times? Jesus saith unto him, I say not unto thee, Until seven times: but, Until seventy times seven."* *Matthew 18:21, 22;* *"Take heed to yourselves: If thy brother trespass against thee, rebuke him; and if he repent, forgive him   And if he trespass against thee seven times in a day, and seven times in a day turn again to thee, saying, I repent; thou shalt forgive him. And the apostles said unto the Lord, Increase our faith."* *Luke 17:3-5*

The only way to forgive in such a manner is with godly virtue. The question concerning the quota is certainly an honest one. Seven times per day is absolutely commendable but four hundred and ninety times is unimaginable. Obviously, that is the point. I would have a hard time staying around someone long enough to forgive them four hundred and ninety times. Besides, if we are counting, then we are not forgiving! The requested prayer for increased forgiving faith is profound and without question personally viable.

Why is it that some people will push or provoke to a point that seemingly reaches unforgiveness? We understand that unsaved people will act and react naturally and without recourse to anything spiritual. The true forgiveness test will be challenged from those that should know better. Therefore, the brethren need to be very aware and on guard of those who will contest the feasibility of forgiveness.

> *"Now I beseech you, brethren, mark them which cause divisions and offences contrary to the doctrine which ye have learned; and avoid them. For they that are such serve not our Lord Jesus Christ, but their own belly; and by good words and fair speeches deceive the hearts of the simple." Romans 16:17, 18;*
> *"Brethren, be followers to together of me, and mark them which walk so as ye have us for an ensample. For many walk, of whom I have told you often, and now tell you even weeping, that they are the enemies of the cross of Christ: Whose end is destruction, whose God is their belly, and whose glory is in their*

*shame, who mind earthly things." Philippians
3:17, 19; "And if any man obey not our word
by this epistle, note that man, and have no
company with him, that he may be ashamed.
Yet count him not as an enemy, but admonish
him as a brother." II Thessalonians 3:14, 15*

The enticement of sin is very visible and we are reminded of how contrary people can be in these verses. These so called brethren were divisive, deceptive, destructive and disobedient and were to be marked, avoided, shamed and admonished. In spite of their repulsive character traits, forgiveness is still attainable.

The extent of forgiveness in CHRIST is eternal! Can you be reproached beyond the ability to grant forgiveness? As mentioned earlier, other than for the eternal unbelief decision, the answer is no! Humanly speaking, we can look at a negative action to play both judge and jury. Being in CHRIST reminds us to never forget how much we have been forgiven. The difficulty is to look past the wrong. A selfish focus will never focus on the Saviour. When we allow unforgiveness to control our thoughts, relationships will be broken and seemingly irreparable.

No doubt, you can think of examples of people that have crossed the line towards unforgiveness.

*"It is reported commonly that there is
fornication among you, and such fornication
as is not so much as named among the
Gentiles, that one should have his father's*

wife. And ye are puffed up, and have not rather mourned, that he that hath done this deed might be taken away from among you. For I verily, as absent in body, but present in spirit, have judged already, as though I were present, concerning him that hath so done this deed. In the name of our Lord Jesus Christ, when ye are gathered together, and my spirit, with the power of our Lord Jesus Christ, To deliver such an one unto Satan for the destruction of the flesh, that the spirit may be saved in the day of the Lord Jesus."
I Corinthians 5:1-5

The incestuous sin of fornication was committed. Although the church was indifferent to this gross sin, the Apostle Paul admonishes them to rebuke the immorality and incur discipline. The church lacked the spiritual fortitude to enact judgment but a judgment had to be made. Verse five is a powerful reality to deal with sin. This reproach receives hands off approach unto the grasp of Satan. Destruction is not annihilation but it is the death of the flesh. The spirit of man will either perish ending up with Satan or be saved and end up with GOD. The man in question is given over to reproach no more.

Does this sin of incest justify unforgiveness? Will forgiveness only be warranted when the body is destroyed and death guaranteed? In the second letter to the Corinthian church we see that forgiveness was asked for but not given.

"Sufficient to such a man is this punishment, which was inflicted of many. So that contrariwise ye ought rather to forgive him, and comfort him, lest perhaps such a one should be swallowed up with overmuch sorrow. Wherefore I beseech you that ye would confirm your love toward him. For to this end also did I write, that I might know the proof of you, whether ye be obedient in all things. To whom ye forgive anything, to whom I forgave it, for your sakes forgave I it in the person of Christ: Lest Satan should get an advantage of us: for we are not ignorant of his devices." II Corinthians 2:6-11

Since punishment was inflicted and repentance followed, forgiveness should be applied. The church's refusal to forgive the man was evident in his discomfort and "overmuch sorrow". Evidently, the man could not move pass the guilt because the church did not confirm him in love. When we sin, the Holy Spirit convicts but never condemns. The product of unforgiveness is condemnation and condemnation is of the devil. "Overmuch sorrow" is a result of not being forgiven but, love shown will prove true forgiveness!

Recognition and repentance of sin is crucial and being restored is the victory. Since we are forgiven in the person of JESUS CHRIST, then the unforgiveness snare should never entangle us.

What's The Bible Got To Do With It?

"Lest Satan should get an advantage of us;
for we are not ignorant of his devices."
II Corinthians 2:11

Unforgiveness is like a cancer and it will engulf your life with bitterness. We must realize that when we hold back forgiveness, we give an advantage to Satan. Unforgiveness is unwarranted and unwise.

What about forgiving yourself? Is it really necessary to receive forgiveness and then remember to forgive yourself for the need to be forgiven? One of the greatest stories in the Bible about forgiveness and restoration is found in Genesis.

"And when Joseph's brethren saw that their father was dead, they said, Joseph will peradventure hate us, and will certainly requite us all the evil which we did unto him. And they sent a messenger unto Joseph, saying, Thy father did command before he died saying, So shall ye say unto Joseph, Forgive, I pray thee now, the trespass of thy brethren, and their sin; for they did unto thee evil: and now, we pray thee, forgive the trespass of the servants of the God of thy father. And Joseph wept when they spake unto him. And his brethren also went and fell down before his face; and they said, Behold, we be thy servants. And Joseph said unto them, Fear not: for am I in the place of God? But as for you, ye thought evil against me; but

*God meant it unto good, to bring to pass as it
is this day, to save much people alive. Now
therefore fear ye not: I will nourish you, and
your little ones. And he comforted them, and
spake kindly unto them." Genesis 50:15-21*

The context leading up to this confrontation is very
profound. Joseph was sold and left for dead by his brothers
but God used Joseph to provide for the nation of Israel. The
Sovereignty of God sheds light on a deep seated principle
between victory and shame. When Jacob died, Joseph's
brothers substantiated a misunderstanding of his great
victory over their rejection and hate. The brothers contrived
a plan to force Joseph's forgiveness toward them. Joseph
had won the magnificent victory years before, but his
brethren never forgave themselves. After years of guilt
ridden shame, finally, restoration was experienced! Evil can
never win when GOD means it for good.

When one really understands the value of forgiveness
over the vanity of unforgiveness, an abundance of life will be
self-permeating. Receiving forgiveness is overwhelmingly
precious but to reciprocate forgiveness is equally infectious.
Joseph was given a choice to let his circumstance make him
or break him.

*"And unto Joseph were born two sons before
the years of famine came which Asenath the
daughter of Poti-pherah priest of On bare
unto him And Joseph called the name of the
firstborn Manasseh: For God, said he, hath*

175

made me forget all my toil, and all my father's house. And the name of the second called he Ephraim: For God hath caused me to be fruitful in the land of my affliction." Genesis 41:50-52

After the discretion and wisdom of Joseph was divulged, Pharaoh gave Joseph a wife. Joseph had two sons named Manasseh (forgetting) and Ephraim (fruitful). In those moments, before ever seeing his father's house, Joseph delineated forgiveness. Joseph would not be bound by animosity or bitterness and he removed the pain that would be prevalent. Because Joseph was able to forgive and forget, he rejoiced in the providential victory! Joseph was left for dead but he lived. He was unjustly accused and unfairly imprisoned but walked out unscathed to experience spiritual fruit. Forgiveness is an awesome choice!

RELATE-

How do you really live out forgiveness? I believe the key is to constantly strive to learn from every opportunity to demonstrate forgiveness.

"But I would ye should understand, brethren, that the things which happened unto me have fallen out rather unto the furtherance of the gospel:" Philippians 1:12; "If others be partakers of this power over you, are not we rather? Nevertheless we have not used this

power; but suffer all things, lest we should hinder the gospel of Christ."
I Corinthians 9:12

Furtherance and hindrance are two defining words with very distinct differences. The gospel is still good news. I can either be influenced toward or against proclaiming the gospel. If my attention is distracted from the gospel, then that distraction has become a hindrance. My desire is to let my attention focus on the furtherance of the gospel. Unforgiveness is a huge obstacle that will squelch any desire to share the good news. Years ago I determined, on purpose, to let *"things which happened unto me"* be unto the furtherance for the gospel in my life.

Like King David, our personal effectiveness will be dictated from our attitude concerning forgiveness.

> *"Have mercy upon me, O God, according to thy loving kindness: according unto the multitude of thy tender mercies blot out my transgressions. Wash me thoroughly from mine iniquity, and cleanse me from my sin. For I acknowledge my transgressions: and my sin is ever before me. Against thee, thee only, have I sinned, and done this evil in thy sight: that thou mightest be justified when thou speakest, and be clear when thou judgest. (1-4); the sacrifices of God are a broken spirit: a broken and a contrite heart, O God, thou wilt not despise. (17); Restore unto me the joy of*

thy salvation; and uphold me with thy free spirit. Then will I teach transgressors thy ways; and sinners shall be converted unto thee." Psalms 51:1-4, 17, 12, 13

This Psalm cuts to the heart and teaches that sin will take anyone to a state of despondency. Because sin is really against the LORD, David is acknowledging his refuge of tender love and full mercy in the LORD. By not blaming society or heredity, he accepted responsibility. Receiving righteous judgment made him understand that the height of contrition far exceeds the death of despair. With his joyful restoration, David relates a tremendous forgiveness principle. His concentration was no longer inward but outward with a desire to help others to be converted. King David let his experience determine his attitude for achievement instead of being dominated by failure.

The Bible speaks about a man named Job. He was a man of integrity, who eschewed evil and feared GOD. The LORD allowed him to live through more difficulties than probably you and I could ever imagine. Through these amazing challenges, Job manifested some wonderful GOD given character traits. Job demonstrates that character is not only who you are, but who you become! Job lived through the cliché *"With friends like this, who needs enemies"*, but he was able to manifest a depth of relating forgiveness that he never understood before.

"Then Job answered and said, I have heard many such things: miserable comforters are

ye all"; "And it was so, that after the LORD had spoken these words unto Job, the LORD said to Eliphaz the Temanite, My wrath is kindled against thee, and against thy two friends: for ye have not spoken of me the thing that is right, as my servant Job hath. Therefore take unto you now seven bullocks and seven rams, and go to my servant Job, and offer up for yourselves a burnt-offering; and my servant Job shall pray for you: for him will I accept: lest I deal with you after your folly, in that ye have not spoken of me the thing which is right, like my servant Job. So Eliphaz the Temanite and Bildad the Shuhite and Zophar the Naamathite went, and did according as the LORD commanded them: the LORD also accepted Job. And the LORD turned the captivity of Job, when he prayed for his friends: also the LORD gave Job twice as much as he had before."
Job 16:1, 2; 42:7-10

Although Job questioned his well-intentioned friends' sincerity, the LORD used him to be a part of their restitution. It was not acceptable for Job to disavow his friends in disgust, but to deal with them through prayer. When we are treated with indifference, instead of responding in like manner, a powerful principle is accomplished when we can look beyond a situation and see the opportunity to pray for

179

the individual(s). There is no reason to be bound or held captive to any problem. Until forgiveness is granted, I highly doubt that prayer will be lifted for an individual. Praying for his friends was the turning point in Job's life that yielded tremendous benefits for everyone. Is it possible that the very act against us is an opening for us to relate forgiveness? Are we willing?

Have you ever been in a situation where your boss or an authoritative person has abused his position? Forgiveness becomes increasingly difficult to fathom as you continue to wait for an appointed time to get back..... oh, I mean forgive!

> *"And the women answered one another as they played, and said, Saul hath slain his thousands, and David his ten thousands. And Saul was very wroth, and the saying displeased him; and he said, They have ascribed unto David ten thousands, and to me they have ascribed but thousands: and what can he have more but the kingdom? And Saul eyed David from that day and forward. And it came to pass on the morrow, that the evil spirit from God came upon Saul, and he prophesied in the midst of the house: and David played with his hand, as at other times: and there was a javelin in Saul's hand. And Saul cast the javelin; for he said, I will smite David even to the wall with it. And David avoided out of his presence twice. And Saul*

was afraid of David, because the LORD was with him, and was departed from Saul. Therefore Saul removed him from him, and made him his captain over a thousand; and he went out and came in before the people. And David behaved himself wisely in all his ways; and the LORD was with him. Wherefore when Saul saw that he behaved himself very wisely, he was afraid of him." "And the evil spirit from the LORD was upon Saul, as he sat in his house with his javelin in his hand: and David played with his hand. And Saul sought to smite David even to the wall with the javelin; but he slipped away out of Saul's presence, and he smote the javelin into the wall: and David fled, and escaped that night." I Samuel 18:7-15; 19:9, 10

This animosity meets virtuosity scenario is a great lesson for all mankind. King Saul utilized David's harp playing skills to calm his nerves. Besides playing, David was a well-known valiant warrior. When the women lauded the military prowess of David, King Saul's pride was hurt. Saul's rage overpowered the serenity he felt from David's harp and he sought out to kill his former appeaser. David was no longer favorable to the king because he felt threatened by him. It is amazing what pride, animosity and jealousy can become even when integrity, prudence and wisdom are prevalent.

What's The Bible Got To Do With It?

*"And he came to the sheepcotes by the way,
where was a cave; and Saul went in to cover
his feet: and David and his men remained in
the sides of the cave. And the men of David
said unto him, Behold the day of which the
LORD said unto thee, Behold, I will deliver
thine enemy into thine hand, that thou mayest
do to him as it shall seem good unto thee.
Then David arose, and cut off the skirt of
Saul's robe privily. And it came to pass
afterward, that David's heart smote him,
because he had cut off Saul's skirt. And he
said unto his men, The LORD forbid that I
should do this thing unto my master, the
LORD's anointed, to stretch forth mine hand
against him, seeing he is the anointed of the
LORD. So David stayed his servants with
these words, and suffered them not to rise
against Saul. But Saul rose up out of the
cave, and went on his way. David also arose
afterward, and went out of the cave, and cried
after Saul, saying, My lord the king. And
when Saul looked behind him, David stooped
with his face to the earth, and bowed himself.
And David said to Saul, Wherefore hearest
thou men's words, saying, Behold, David
seeketh thy hurt? Behold, this day thine eyes
have seen how that the LORD had delivered
thee to day into mine hand in the cave: and*

some bade me kill thee: but mine eye spared thee; and I said, I will not put forth mine hand against my lord; for he is the LORD's anointed.; David said furthermore, As the LORD liveth, the LORD shall smite him; or his day shall come to die; or he shall descend into battle, and perish. The LORD forbid that I should stretch for the mine hand, against the LORD's anointed: but, I pray thee, take thou now the spear that is at his bolster, and the cruse of water, and let us go."
I Samuel 24:3-10; 26:10, 11

To relate forgiveness after the treatment that David received is quite extraordinary. When the opportunity for vengeance presented itself, even under his men's influence, David declined to inflict harm against the anointed king. To many people, David would have been justified to respond in like manner; however, he did not succumb to this mindset.

How often have you and I been confronted with a similar circumstance? Murder probably was not on your mind, but a vehement anger toward someone captivated you. When you spend enough time around someone, familiarity can breed disgust which can become a personality conflict. One may even be annoyed by certain gestures or mannerisms. The question that needs to be asked is *"Why does these certain character traits bother or affect me in a negative way?"* David was not yet the king, but would pride, animosity and jealousy become him? Is it possible that the reason David did not retaliate is because his own character flaws were on display? The LORD can put a boss, teacher, co-worker, family member, etc; in our life to show us who we are and how we can be annoying ourselves. It is quite revealing to realize that the lesson we need to learn the best is the very thing that we loathe the most. Understanding that retaliation and vengeance is never right makes relating forgiveness so liberating!

> *"And be ye kind one to another, tenderhearted, forgiving one another, even as God for Christ's sake hath forgiven you." Ephesians 4:32; "Forbearing one another, and forgiving one another, if any many have a quarrel against any: even as Christ forgave you, so also do ye." Colossians 3:13*

Yes, dealing with humans will always have an endless state of affairs that will challenge anyone. How much greater is it to relate kindness instead of hate, be tenderhearted instead of unloving and reveal forbearance instead of a quick temper? To be prepared for every situation is hardly plausible, but applying these practical attributes will definitely help.

> *"And whatsoever ye do, do it heartily, as to the LORD, and not unto men: knowing that of the LORD ye shall receive the reward of the inheritance: for ye serve the LORD Christ." Colossians 3:23, 24*

If we approach life with this attitude, I believe the ability to be offended will be non-existent. If everything is done as unto the LORD, it will not matter how people respond, receive, appreciate or give thanks, etc. We will not expect anything nor make anyone uphold a set of predetermined standard reactions. This approach will relinquish any ill feelings and receive the LORD's reward. These verses have helped me tremendously in my relationship skills. When I am not looking to be offended or wondering when I will be offended, I can look beyond the statement or reaction and let it go. It is very easy to relate forgiveness when you are not offended, Amen!

I am pronouncing an open invitation for anyone to join the *"Be Spent Club"*. I coined this term to attract members. It is a great biblical club but there are very few members.

"And I will very gladly spend and be spent for
you; though the more abundantly I love you,
the less I be loved." II Corinthians 12:15

"I will" is an awesome statement to demonstrate the difference between availability and ability. Those with the ability are not always given to availability. This is a conscious proactive desire when dealing with people. *"Very gladly"* is an attitude that is second to none. When "glad" is in your conversation and lifestyle, then you will be grateful and fulfilled regardless of the results. *"Spend and be spent for you"* will provoke you to evaluate your assets. Unfortunately, we weigh the costs over the load of benefits.

What's The Bible Got To Do With It?

We seem to ask questions such as how much time do I spend, how sincere is the person and will it really do any good? These are viable questions however; they should not be asked to escape the opportunity to help someone, but rather to figure out what it will take to accomplish the desired result. To be expended is an individual prerogative therefore, personal involvement will incur cost. This reminds me of an eighty year old man that told me *"The easiest way to do a job is to let somebody else do it."* That statement may try to justify a way out, but we know that humans are a mess and require a lot of work and there is no easy way out. Although spending money is sometimes easier than spending time, to *"be spent"* is to go a little farther even unto exhaustion. Are you ready to join the club yet? *"Though the more abundantly I love you"* is beyond the adequate or "just enough" love. The commitment to more abundant love is profound especially when there is no final calculation. *"The less I be loved"* is not the reaction that you would expect from someone receiving your help. If your motive for showing love is to receive love, then you will probably be hurt. Unconditional love never needs to be reciprocated. When applied to your life, this truth will profoundly enhance your forgiving ability. Each day new and unique opportunities will be available to prove your willingness to remain a member of the *"Be Spent Club"*. My wife framed this verse for me and I read it every day.

Forgiveness is a subject of great depth, but I am abounding in gratitude to rejoice because of forgiveness. I reckon myself forgiven in order to receive and reciprocate forgiveness and it is with great pleasure to relate forgiveness day by day!

What's The Bible Got To Do With It?

FOUNDATION

The dictionary says that "foundation" means the basis or lowest part of a structure, the ground work, the principles or origin of anything.[1] Man certainly has his opinion but I believe that the Bible is the foundation of everything! The test of time continues to prove the Bible and everything that has been predicted has come to pass. I believe you and I should give heed to everything that is yet predicted will come to pass. I am not sure why there are so many skeptics or others that uphold disdain toward the Bible. What is there to be afraid of? Is the Bible just another book that we can dismiss because of disagreement or does the number one best-selling book have some information that brings value to life? We all have the ability to agree or disagree. If the Bible is truly God's Word and God tells us who He is and who we are through His Word, then we might want to reconsider our dismissal!

In my life the Bible has been foundational for my guidance and it continues to be paramount for my decisions.

> *"All scripture is given by the inspiration of God, and is profitable for doctrine, for reproof, for correction, for instruction in righteousness:" II Tim 3:16.*

This verse has helped me in decisions to know what is right, what is wrong, how to make it right, and how to stay right.

> *"Thy Word is a lamp unto my feet and a light unto my path" Ps 119:105. "Except the LORD build the house, they labour in vain that build it: except the LORD keep the city, the watchmen waketh but in vain". Psalms 127:1*

These verses have helped me tremendously when I was without a direction to train up the five children that our LORD gave us. Like a flashlight in the night that is pointed directly forward, we can be confident to make decisions with a watchman's eye. Can we really expect to make a house a home without the instructor's blueprint? Many examples and principles for life, such as how to raise a family, are in the Bible so why would we not learn from others mistakes and accomplishments? We are bombarded on all sides to only react from a human perspective, but the Bible has a totally different outlook with a godly perspective. The Bible never sugar coats the frailty of man nor covers up his sin. King David is one of the most known characters in the Bible, but there are as many positive aspects about his life as there are negative. We are given an observation and an overview of man's greatest and most egregious accomplishments. Through the mirror of biblical truth we can understand and apply the scriptures. We have a bottom line and an unquestionable plumb line for life!

"Trust in the LORD with all thine heart; and lean not unto thine own understanding. In all thy ways acknowledge him, and he shall direct thy paths" Proverbs 3:5, 6

Memorizing these two verses has given me great consolation in the provision of God! It is not a blind trust nor will our understanding lack stability. Confidence in the Lord will ensure good understanding. Regardless of the situation, no matter what is happening in my life, wherever I am, without a doubt I can avow the LORD. His power and presence is declared through His word and He will conduct our steps in straight order!

"The LORD is my shepherd; I shall not want" Psalms 23:1.

Have you ever had the feeling of loneliness or fear? We can be assured of the overwhelming care and concern that the Shepherd of the sheep has for them. When I start to think that I don't have anything or that I am missing something, the sweet calming memory of this verse touches my heart and floods me with comfort.

The Sufficing Bible
When I am tired, the Bible is my bed;
Or in the dark, the Bible is my light.
When I am hungry, it is vital bread;
Or fearful, it is armor for the fight.
When I am sick, 'tis healing medicine;

What's The Bible Got To Do With It?

Or lonely, thronging friends I find therein.

If I would work, the Bible is my tool;
Or play, it is a harp of happy sound.
If I am ignorant, it is my school;
If I am sinking, it is solid ground.
If I am cold, the Bible is my fire;
And wings, if boldly I aspire.

Should I be lost, the Bible is my guide;
Or naked, it is raiment, rich and warm.
Am I imprisoned it is ranges wide;
Or tempest-tossed, a shelter from the storm.
Would I adventure, 'tis a gallant sea;
Or would I rest, it is a flowery lea.

Does gloom oppress? The Bible is a sun.
Or ugliness? It is a garden fair.
Am I athirst? How cool its currents run!
Or stifled? What a vivifying air!
Since thus thou givest of thyself to me.
How should I give myself, great Book, to thee!

Amos R. Wells[2]

> *"For all flesh is as grass, and all the glory of man as the flower of grass. The grass withereth, and flower thereof falleth away:*

But the Word of the Lord endureth for ever..." I Peter 1:24, 25.

The Bible is the incontestable, incorruptible, indestructible and indispensable Word of God. No one can argue with it and nothing can corrupt it. Nothing can destroy it and nothing can replace it as the source and wellspring of life. Through sheer longevity and infallible truth my foundation is established with the Word of God. As you can see, the Bible has everything to do with my life.

"For other foundation can no man lay than that is laid, which is JESUS CHRIST" I Corinthians 3:11

There is no other foundation for life that has merit. The eternal established base cannot be excavated nor the support shaken. I mentioned a verse from Second Timothy in the beginning of this chapter that speaks of the inspiration of God. Many people think that mere men have written the Bible, but the idea that man alone wrote the Bible is ludicrous. Getting forty people over a 1600 year period to agree in text about the same thing without error is preposterous. Furthermore, man is not smart enough nor that agreeable. Besides, man would never condemn himself because he would then need to admit his need of a Saviour. The Bible says that he who does not believe is condemned already.

What's The Bible Got To Do With It?

"For God sent not his Son into the world to condemn the world; but that the world through him might be saved." John 3:18

Foundationally then, the Bible is very believable and undeniable. Without question it is transformable because the Word of God has transformed my very being and mindset. I no longer have to live under who I was, but now I live in who the LORD wants me to become! When the LORD becomes your foundation, He will make a change in you too!

"Therefore if any man be in Christ, he is a new creature: old things are passed away; behold, all things are become new." II Corinthians 5:17.

For many years the unbelievers, scoffers, and some scientists have tried to disprove the Bible. Be assured if it were possible, it would be world renowned information. Instead, as previously mentioned, the Bible continues to be the number one sold book in the world. The infallible Word of God is sustainable for me in all ways and is the most durable possession anyone can own.

In addition, my foundation in life is enhanced with many teaching aids from the Bible. It is a geographical, mathematical, archaeological, psychological and prophetical book and last but not least it is historical. No other book will expound on more subjects at the same time. In response to the "that's your interpretation" cliché, I point us to the following verse.

II Peter 1:19-21 "We have also a more sure word of prophecy... Knowing this first, that no prophecy of the scripture is of any private interpretation. For the prophecy came not in old time by the will of man; but holy men of God spake as they were moved by the Holy Ghost."

The apostle Peter is reminding us that physical presence or visibility does not outweigh our confidence in the written Word. We receive application for our life without selfish interpretation. As my pastor years ago told me, *"If literal sense makes good sense, then make no other sense" James Adams.* We answer or prove the Bible with the Bible, scripture upon scripture, whereby we can rightly divide the Word of Truth.

"Study to shew thyself approved unto God, a workman that needeth not to be ashamed, rightly dividing the word of truth." II Timothy 2:15

While I am touching this not so "politically correct" issue, the Bible is very clear and unapologetic toward the right to life and that life begins at conception with a sin nature.

"Behold, I was shapen in iniquity; and in sin did my mother conceive me." Psalms 51:5, "My substance was not hid from thee, when I was made in secret, and curiously wrought in

the lowest parts of the earth." "Thine eyes did see my substance, yet being unperfect; and in thy book all my members were written, which in continuance were fashioned, when as yet there was none of them." Psalms 139:15, 16; "Before I formed thee in the belly I knew thee; and before thou camest forth out of the womb I sanctified thee, and I ordained thee a prophet unto the nations." Jeremiah 1:5, "But when it pleased God, who separated me from my mother's womb, and called me by his grace." Galatians 1:15

One more foundational truth is that the sanctity of marriage is and always will be between one man and one woman.

"Therefore shall a man leave his father and mother, and shall cleave, unto his wife: and they shall be one flesh" Genesis 2:24.

Anything else is contrary to God's Word and will subject society to moral anguish.

My Foundation for life is the Bible. What is yours?

FRIENDSHIP

Have you ever finished a phone conversation and said *"I have not talked with him for years, but it was like we had just spoken yesterday"*? I have experienced this statement in my life. Would this be classified as a true friendship? It has been said that if in one life time you can say you have had five friends, then you have lived a blessed life! Amazingly, I believe that this statement is true. Many friends "come and go" but the one that loves you anyway, regardless, no matter what, is really your friend. Can you count your friends on one hand?

I try to live with a motto that says, "A person that I don't know is a friend I haven't met." Although I have several ideas about true friendship, I know that the Bible has a better idea.

> *"These things have I spoken unto you, that my joy might remain in you, and that your joy might be full. This is my commandment, That ye love one another, as I have loved you. Greater love hath no man than this, that a man lay down his life for his friends. Ye are my friends, if ye do whatsoever I command you. Henceforth I call you not servants; for*

the servant knoweth not what his lord doeth:
but I have called you friends; for all things
that I have heard of my Father I have made
known unto you." John 15:11-15

Jesus is relating a truth about the basis and the responsibility of friendship. Joy comes from an acceptance that we are pleasing to someone. Certainly, joy reigns in your life when you heed God's Word. I believe true friendship will be involved with others that abide therein. We all have acquaintances and co-workers that we call friends, but not all are deep, fond friends. Of course, we love our friends but laying down our lives for our friends is a whole lot deeper and more serious thought. We live in a social environment and who we are will attract others. People who are God's friends will hear and obey His commandments! Do we attract this kind of friend?

"Choose your friends wisely" is an interesting cliché. Friends are very influential and they can be very controlling. Because of both positive and negative influences, we know that friends can either make you or break you. Friends can either be a help or a hindrance in your life.

"Ye adulterers and adulteresses, know ye not
that the friendship of the world is enmity with
God? Whosoever therefore will be a friend of
the world is the enemy of God." James 4:4

This verse relates a very strong truth. There is a friend and an enemy with God. These two facets are diametrically opposed to one another. We know that one cannot be both nor play both sides. Adultery is usually stated with a sexual connotation but here it used against co-mingling the world and God. The world system, thoughts, ideas, direction, etc. is no friend with God. The world owns three dictates that are declared in First John chapter two and verse sixteen.

> *"For all that is in the world, the lust of the flesh, and lust of the eyes, and the pride of life, is not of the Father, but is of the world."*

If my friendship to God is real, then my friendship with the world cannot be real. Therefore my human social friends must be on the same page and join in the same journey.

We are told that Abraham was called *"the friend of God" (James 2:23).* This verse reveals a tremendous caricature of his testimony. I want to strive for that same character trait and seek those that are like minded.

> *"A man that hath friends must shew himself friendly: and there is a friend that sticketh closer that a brother" Proverbs 18:24*

This verse shows the availability and accountability of friendship. Too many lack friendly expressiveness in order to acquire or enjoy more friends but, JESUS will never leave us alone. It is unfortunate that even the best of friends can become fickle. True friends will listen, be available and stand with you come what may. However, when a little admonition is given out of love, it seems that too many flee with an offended heart.

> *"Faithful are the wounds of a friend; but the kisses of an enemy are deceitful. Iron sharpeneth iron: so a man sharpeneth the countenance of his friend." Proverbs 27:6, 17*

We have all been led down an ulterior motive pathway but, a true friend will tell you the truth. A friend will tell what you need to hear and not just what you want to hear! A faithful wound with love is much more useful than a patronizing kiss. We need a friend who will lift us up when we are right and stand up when we are wrong. Too many people carry their feelings on their shoulders and get hurt without understanding the true value of a friend. A true friend can rub you the wrong way but, you know that being "cut to the heart" is for your own good. If your countenance is affected, you probably just need to get over yourself and get a grip! It is wonderful to have a friend that is only motivated to benefit others through speaking the truth!

Friends share their deepest emotions, feelings and tender moments. This information is not open for public discourse. Any friend that reveals such delicate information is considered a gossiper.

> *"A forward man soweth strife: and whisperer separateth chief friends. He that covereth a transgression seeketh love; but he that repeateth a matter separateth very friends." Proverbs 16:28; 17:9*

These two verses demonstrate a closeness and security that friends enjoy but also a severe divide that can exist! When a person confides in his friend, the bond of friendship will keep that conversation in confidence.

Again, our choice of friends is vitally important. If someone has ulterior motives, they can say the right words and do the right things and still in the end turn on you. This principle shows up in Psalms 41:9 and Psalms 55:12, 13.

> *"Yea, mine own familiar friend, in whom I trusted, which did eat of my bread, hath lifted up his heel against me. For it was not an enemy that reproached me; then I could have borne it: neither was it he that hated me that did magnify himself against me; then I would have hid myself from him: but it was thou, a man mine equal, my guide, and mine acquaintance."*

The Psalmist David is unloading his heart concerning people, entrusted people, which turned on him. We normally do not stay upset when someone we do not know gets an attitude against us but, when our friend or close acquaintance turns on us; it is very different and much more hurtful. We generally hold confidence and trust in high regard and when that is stepped on, it magnifies the emotional injury.

> *"And the same day Pilate and Herod were made friends together: for before they were at enmity between themselves." Luke 23.12*

What's The Bible Got To Do With It?

It is amazing what vehement hatred our LORD received and how a visceral camaraderie made enemies to become friends. The old cliché, "Keep your friends close and your enemies closer" is very thought provoking. Our LORD JESUS CHRIST was betrayed to the epitome of the word and maybe this is why he called Judas Iscariot his *"friend" (Matthew 26:50)*! To what extent should the bounds of our friendship be?

Probably the most classic biblical friendship example we have is found in the Book of First Samuel chapter eighteen. The friendship covenant between Jonathan and David is second to none. Although Jonathan was heir to the throne, we know that David would one day be king. Jealousy and animosity lifted up its ugly head in King Saul, but Jonathan never allowed his pride or prestige to influence him against David. These true friends purposed to keep and cherish their friendship no matter what happened. To their very being (soul) they protected the covenant relationship.

As I get older, I am reminded of the wisdom that is available from those with a hoary head.

> *"Thine own friend, and thy father's friend, forsake not..." Proverbs 27:10*

We have established a friendship with the older generation. Because of this relationship it keeps us from repeating the same mistakes. Also, by their insight we can enjoy what they experienced. I have special memories of wonderful conversations with my grandparents, parents, in-laws and their friends inclusively. As life goes on and experience grows, one can glean advantages from friendships of old. Our ministry has been involved with many building projects. We have benefited from retired professionals that have shared advice for efficiency and expediency. What a blessing it is to learn from their experiences. To disavow or negate these friendships would be detrimental.

Of course, everyone knows not to burn your bridges, right? King David kept his attitude about friendships real and true. When the opportunity to bless the descendants of Jonathan was known, Mephibosheth (Jonathan's son) became a recipient of the kindness and sweet knowledge of past friendships. Although he had nothing to offer in return, Mephibosheth dined at the king's table all his days (II Samuel 9:1-13)!

Is it really about having a vast quantity of friends or about having quality friendships?

> *"Wealth maketh many friends, but the poor is separated from his neighbour. A false witness shall not be unpunished, and he that speaketh lies shall not escape. Many will intreat the favour of the prince: and every man is a friend to him that giveth gifts. All the brethren of the poor do hate him: how much more do his friends go far from him? He pursueth them with words, yet they are wanting to him" Proverbs 19:4-7*

Wealth attracts people and those less wealthy seem unattractive. People that only base their friendships by what they can get from others, will never be a true friend. When being selfishly motivated by money is the only criteria for friendship, be assured that when the money runs out, the "friend" will be gone. If friendship is based on anything other than human interaction, being a blessing, camaraderie and companionship, the poor will be friendship deficient.

> *"And he said unto them, Which of you shall have a friend, and shall go unto him at midnight, and say unto him, Friend, lend me three loaves: for a friend of mine in his journey is come to me, and I have nothing to set before him? And he from within shall answer and say, Trouble me not: the door is now shut, and my children are with me in bed; I cannot rise and give thee. I say unto you, Though he will not rise and give him, because he is his friend, yet because of his importunity he will rise and give him as many as he needeth. And I say unto you, Ask, and it shall begiven you; seek, and ye shall find; knock, and it shall be opened unto you. For every one that asketh receiveth; and he that seeketh findeth; and to him that knocketh it shall be opened." Luke 11:5-10*

This principle reveals why true friendships will look beyond the circumstance or inconvenience. When we need a friend, we contact those that will help regardless of the situation. The friend from within the house was annoyed and only acted on importunity (incessant insistence). He did not understand the opportunity to show forth his friendship; instead, he felt obligated under his friends' persistent request. His guise of friendly support is a striking contrast to true friendly assistance. We are so fortunate to have a friend in JESUS that never feels obligated or is aggravated with us in any situation. Our relationship with Him is open to ask, seek and knock! In CHRIST JESUS, we are afforded opportunities beyond our imagination. With this open door, may our attitude about friendships be authentic and our desire to cultivate more friends genuine.

What's The Bible Got To Do With It?

FUNNY

The Bible has plenty of humor in it. The Bible deals with people and people are quite humorous. Many clichés and sayings are used in modern day vernacular. Few people are aware that certain commonly used phrases come from the Bible.

It is ironic that many people will use these clichés and sayings that come from the Bible, but they will not let the Bible guide their everyday life. The following story will portray a biblical principle using our everyday clichés and sayings that are intertwined throughout the Bible. While using conversational clichés, the story culminates with a serious human need. The biblical references will follow the story and I believe you will enjoy looking them up!

There was an *ambidextrous*[1] man who had *wrinkles*[2] named *Witty*[3] who lived in the *suburbs*[4] and while attending *college*[5] he found a book. He enjoyed living and eating foods that were *half-baked*[6] and *as fat as grease*[7]. As of yet, Witty was not married but, he had a girl *who is spoken for*[8] because she is *the apple of his eye*[9]. The girl's mom is sweet and he always heard that *as is the mother, so is the daughter*[10]. Letting the bond of *mizpah*[11] be their guide and

207

knowing that *two heads are better than one[12];* they plan to marry and share *body heat[13].*

Witty grew up being told to *be a man[14]* but seemed to be *beside himself[15]* living with the motto *every man for himself[16].* After *making his own bed from sleeping in it[17],* Witty began to *rise and shine[18]* early working by *the sweat of his brow[19]* living off *the fat of the land[20]* without an *evil eye[21]* listening to the townsmen let their *money talk[22]* about how *money flies[23]* because *talk is cheap[24].* They told their *trafficking[25]* stories about others who were not *sorry for getting caught[26].* Without *splitting hairs[27],* they murmured that it seems like *crime pays[28]* and that they should have received a *speedy sentence[29]* but, no one wanted to add *fuel to the fire[30]* and that was the *God's honest truth[31].* From *time to time[32]* or *something to that effect[33],* after placing a *beware of dogs[34]* sign on his fence, Witty returned to *kindle a fire[35]* with the townsmen making *much ado about nothing[36]* as they did not *cry over spilt milk[37]* but let all be *water under the bridge[38].* While being pretty much *at their wits end[39],* Witty guided his life by watching the *blind leading the blind[40]* and listened to *old wives fables[41]* as he searched the *post office[42]* waiting for news in order to say *a little birdie told me[43].*

One day, Witty's friend *Wisdom[44], who is the spitting image of his father[45],* came to visit him and not by *happenstance[46]* he saw the book sitting on the *mantle[47]* that Witty had found. Wisdom *straight up[48]* asked Witty, *choosing his words wisely[49],* to read it because it is the Bible. Although Witty knew his life like the *back of his hand[50]* and he realized that *there is nothing new under the sun[51],* he did not *see eye to eye*[52] with Wisdom but, he would not *talk behind his back*[53]. Witty made a face like he had *eaten sour grapes*[54] and said "All that is a *drop in a bucket*"[55]. Even though his *ears tingled*[56], Witty *railed on*[57] Wisdom to *hold his peace*[58]. Because Wisdom *made him ill*[59], Witty said "*Good riddance*"[60].

Witty was *breaking the heart*[61] of Wisdom but, rather than sounding *holier than thou*[62] and *giving him his due*[63], Wisdom didn't *wash his hands of the matter*[64] but said "*Mark my words*"[65] and "I can not *take back my words*"[66] and remembered that *what goes around comes around*[67].

Although Witty was *quick on his feet*[68] and knowing that *haste makes waste*[69], he cut himself through *flesh and bones*[70] and laid there *half-dead*[71]. It was *no small stir*[72] upon arriving *safe and sound*[73] at the hospital. While *tossing to and fro*[74] lying in the hospital bed, Witty *little by little*[75] began to think about what Wisdom had said *putting his neck out for him*[76]. After the hospital *gave him leave*[77] and because of Wisdom's *witness*[78], Witty became *speechless*[79] knowing that his life was *upside down*[80] and with *knocking knees*[81], *his hair stood up*[82], *setting his teeth on edge*[83]. Even in his *best state*[84] Witty said "I *reckon*[85] it is *high time*[86]" knowing that the *writing is on the wall*[87] and that this is *the time and season*[88] to *escape by the skin of my teeth*[89].

In the end, *before meeting his maker*[90], Witty came *face to face*[91] with himself and got *born again*[92] to *fight the good fight of faith*[93] with Wisdom. Shortly after putting his *house in order*[94], Witty *gave up the ghost*[95] and they *cast a cloth upon him*[96]. May the ending truth of this story be that *history repeats itself*[97] in every one!

1. I CHRONICLES 12:2
2. JOB 16:8
3. PROVERBS 8:12
4. EZEKIEL 27:28
5. II CHRONICLES 34:22
6. HOSEA 7:8
7. PSALMS 119:70
8. SONG OF SOLOMON 8:8
9. DEUTERONOMY 32:10
10. EZEKIEL 16:44
11. GENESIS 31:49
12. ECCLESIASTES 4:9
13. ECCLESIASTES 4:11
14. JOB 38:3
15. MARK 3:21
16. NUMBERS 31:53
17. ISAIAH 28:20
18. ISAIAH 60.1
19. GENESIS 3:19
20. GENESIS 45:18
21. PROVERBS 23:6
22. ECCLESIASTES 10:19
23. PROVERBS 23:5
24. PROVERBS 14:23
25. EZEKIEL 28:18
26. JEREMIAH 2:26
27. JUDGES 20:16
28. ECCLESIASTES 8:11
29. ECCLESIASTES 8:11
30. EZEKIEL 21:32
31. ROMANS 3:4
32. I CHRONICLES 9:25
33. II CHRONICLES 34:22
34. PHILIPPIANS 3:2
35. EZEKIEL 24:10
36. MARK 5:39
37. II SAMUEL 14:14
38. JOB 11:16
39. PSALMS 107:27
40. MATTHEW 15:14
41. I TIMOTHY 4:7
42. ESTHER 8:10
43. ECCLESIASTES 10:20
44. PROVERBS 8:12
45. HEBREWS 1:3
46. RUTH 2:3
47. I KINGS 19:13
48. GENESIS 43.7
49. JOB 9:14
50. ISAIAH 49:16
51. ECCLESIASTES 1:9
52. ISAIAH 52:8

53. I KINGS 14:9
54. JEREMIAH 31:29
55. ISAIAH 40:15
56. I SAMUEL 3:11
57. II CHRONICLES 32:17
58. II KINGS 2:3
59. PSALMS 106:32
60. ZEPHANIAH 1:18
61. ACTS 21:13
62. ISAIAH 65:5
63. I CHRONICLES 16:29
64. MATTHEW 27:24
65. JOB 18:2
66. ISAIAH 31:2
67. PROVERBS 26:27
68. II SAMUEL 2:18
69. PROVERBS 21:5
70. II SAMUEL 19:12
71. LUKE 10:30
72. ACTS 12:18
73. LUKE 15:27
74. JOB 7:4
75. EXODUS 23:30
76. ROMANS 16:4
77. JOHN 19:38
78. ACTS 1:8
79. MATTHEW 22:12
80. ACTS 17:6

81. DANIEL 5:6
82. JOB 4:15
83. JEREMIAH 31:29
84. PSALMS 39:5
85. ROMANS 6:11
86. ROMANS 13:11
87. DANIEL 5:5
88. ECCLESIASTES 3:1
89. JOB 19:20
90. PROVERBS 22:2
91. PROVERBS 27:19
92. JOHN 3:3
93. I TIMOTHY 6:12
94. II KINGS 20:1
95. JOHN 19:30
96. II SAMUEL 20:12
97. ECCLESIASTES 1:9

FUTURE

The Bible foretells that there will be those that mock, scorn and ridicule in the last days (II Peter 3:3, 4). I contest that we have been living in the final days since the days of JESUS CHRIST!

> *"God, who at sundry times and in divers manners spake in time past unto the fathers by the prophets, Hath in these last days spoken unto us by his Son, whom he hath appointed heir of all things, by whom also he made the worlds;" Hebrews 1:1,2*

Since the Bible explains that the end times will be perilous times (II Timothy 3:1), why are we surprised to be living in them?

The Bible reveals a very explicit world and human view, but also a personal view. A future view is quite prevalent for each. Everything after chapter three in the Book of Revelation is still future. The Church (Body of Christ) is yet to be complete. In First Thessalonians 4:13-18 a marvelous phenomenon is taught concerning the Church that will one day rapture (be caught up) into the clouds. The world will enter Daniel's prophetic seventieth week time line called the Tribulation period and seven years will ensue. It is sad that our society misuses the term "Armageddon", but the Bible very precisely defines the "Battle of Armageddon" and depicts the place the battle will occur (Zechariah 12:11; Revelation 16:14-16). The battle will finalize the tribulation period and precede the one thousand year Millennial Reign of JESUS CHRIST (Revelation 20:4, 5)!

Humanity should not be ignorant of the coming turmoil or be amazed when it overwhelms those that remain post rapture. The eventual precursor to these concise biblical events is apostasy and apathy. Too many humans are oblivious to these "signs of the times".

Personally, my future "take" on the Bible is how it applies to me. It is a future book because my life and everyone else's life is portrayed in it.

> *"For thou hast possessed my reins: thou hast covered me in my mother's womb. I will praise thee; for I am fearfully and wonderfully made: marvelous are thy works; and that my soul knoweth right well. My substance was not hid from thee, when I was made in secret, and curiously wrought in the lowest parts of the earth. Thine eyes did see my substance, yet being unperfect; and in thy book all my members were written, which in continuance were fashioned, when as yet there was none of them. How precious also*

are thy thoughts unto me, O God! How great is the sum of them!" Psalms 139:13-17

These verses teach us that the Lord knew us in the womb. Although He never forces anything on us, He does know our future. Upon coming to an age of accountability and upon responding to the drawing power of God, a person can receive or reject His plan for his/her life. God loves us and always has our best interest for His glory in mind. We were created for the Lord's good pleasure and He has established our life before the foundation of the world. In the end, after your life, each person will spend eternity in one of the two future biblical destinies. Each saved person has a future with the Lord and conversely each unsaved person has a future without the Lord.

> *"Being confident of this very thing, that he which hath begun a good work in you will perform it until the day of Jesus Christ:"*
> *Philippians 1:6*

A powerful truth unfolds before us as we understand that our future is known to the Lord and it is laid out before us. Upon receiving Jesus Christ, we are assured that the best plan began in our decision to be saved. His will is then performed through us until we go to our future home to be with our Lord!

I was not born with this understanding but when I was born again I then began to understand. The future that my Lord has for me continues to be revealed day by day. I am thankful for every future opportunity that is yet known to me. My life before being saved was a preparation and precursor for my life in Christ! Oh the joy to live out the experience of my wife, our children, the call to the ministry and a love for missions that has been given to me! I am in great expectation to live out the promises that are written but yet future for me.

> *"Call unto me, and I will answer thee, and shew thee great and mighty things, which thou knowest not." Jeremiah 33:3*

This is one of the most exciting verses in the Bible concerning the future. Our days are numbered, and I want to live them to the fullest. I love the imagination that this verse exemplifies. In Christ, we have so much at our disposal and it is a shame not to enjoy all that our future holds. His specific will for each life has both victories and defeats, blessings and hard lessons, but all will be a benefit. No matter what we are confronted with, it should be a compliment to us and not a detriment. Unfortunately, too many people will dwell on the negative aspect and miss the positive aspect. Because every good gift comes from above (James 1:17), then we must know that no trial, struggle, or difficulty is too big or overwhelming to the One that has a plan for our life. If you are not excited about your future blessings, then I challenge you to join His future for you!

We are living under social, economic and political controls that influence us in many different ways, but no matter what, our future is secure. Amongst the uncertainty and chaos, I am more excited than ever. Remember that in Christ we have the future revealed in the back of the Book of Books and we win!

What's The Bible Got To Do With It?

BIBLIOGRAPHY

Alcorn, Randy. *The Treasure Principle.* Sisters, OR: Multnomah Publishers, Inc, 2001.

Amos, R. Wells. *The Collected Poems._* Boston, MA: The Christian Endeavor World, 1921

Longoria, Lyndon. *Stewardship, Treasure.* Strength For Today Ministries, 2009

Rogers, Adrian. *A Future For The Family.* Atlanta, GA: Walk Thru the Bible Ministries, 1996

Webster, Noah. *Webster's New School & Office Dictionary.* New York, NY: Book Enterprises, Inc, 1955

Wiersbe, Warren W. *The Bible Exposition Commentary.* Wheaton, IL: Victor Books, 1989

What's The Bible Got To Do With It?

FOOTNOTES

CHAPTER ONE
1. "Dream". *Webster's New School & Office Dictionary.* New York, NY: Book Enterprises, Inc, 1955

CHAPTER THREE
1. Rogers, D. A. (1996). *A Future For The Family.* (p. 16,17). Atlanta, GA: Walk Thru The Bible Ministries.

2. Wiersbe, W. W. (1989). *The Bible Exposition Commentary.* (Vol. 2, p. 410,411). Wheaton, IL: Victor Books.

CHAPTER FOUR
1. Alcorn, R. (2001). *The Treasure Principle.* (p. 53, 54). Sisters, OR: Multnomah Publishers, Inc.

2. Longoria, L. (2009, February 17). *Stewardship, Treasure.* Strength For Today Ministries.

CHAPTER SIX
1. "Forgive". *Webster's New School & Office Dictionary.* New York, NY: Book Enterprises, Inc, 1955

CHAPTER SEVEN
1. "Foundation". *Webster's New School & Office Dictionary.* New York, NY: Book Enterprises, Inc, 1955
2. Amos, R. W. (1921). *The Collected Poems.* (p. 10). Boston, MA: The Christian Endeavor World.

Our beautiful, blessed
life as missionaries.

Our precious Wedding Day.

Our beautiful, blessed family.

I received my Doctorate in Theology.

A display table in a local church on the Deputation Trail.

Sharing a film in Open Air Meeting.

Praying before a service.

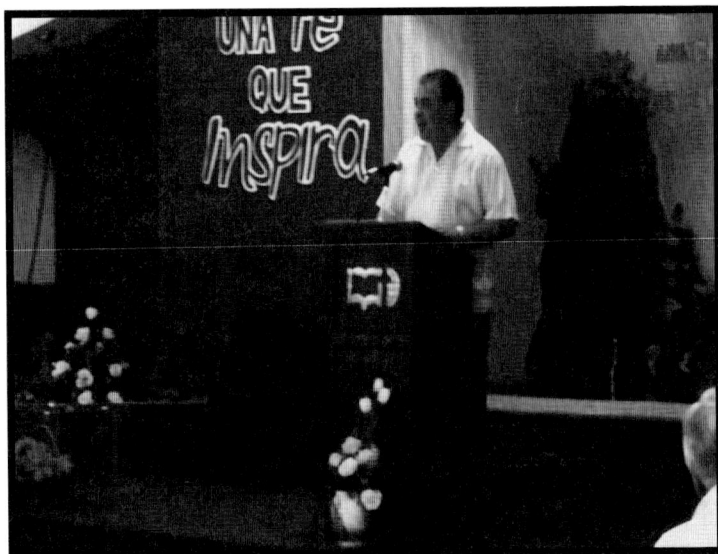

Mission Trip. I was preaching in El Salvador.

Local church Worship Service.

Baptismal Service

Constructing a building in Nuevo Laredo
Tamps, Mexico.

Constructing building for an established local Church.

Constructed building in Laredo, Texas

Working with National Pastors' families.

From our trip to Haiti.

I am a pilot and I flew food back and forth from the Dominican Republic to Haiti . Tammy, my wife, a nurse, worked in a hospital after the earthquake.

Tammy with nurses in Haiti.

Street Preaching in Mexico City.

Kelle Hein

Kelle Hein

Heaven O, because we've said Hell-O for too many years. My wife, Tammy, and I have been married since 1985 and we've been blessed with five wonderful children. We have served as missionaries on the Border of Mexico since 1986. This book came from a desire to continue my education. Upon writing a thesis for my Doctorate, I decided to publish it. I'm very grateful and I humbly thank you for reading my thoughts on the importance that the Bible has been and continues to be in my life. My prayer is that you will be encouraged to let the Word of God guide your life as it does mine!

Shari Parker Publishing

2785 CR 3103

New Boston, Texas 75570

903-933-6273

sharipar@yahoo.com

www.shariparkerpublishingandprinting.co